Alexander John Ellis

Rules and Regulations in Prisons in Ireland

Alexander John Ellis

Rules and Regulations in Prisons in Ireland

ISBN/EAN: 9783741107849

Manufactured in Europe, USA, Canada, Australia, Japa

Cover: Foto ©Suzi / pixelio.de

Manufactured and distributed by brebook publishing software
(www.brebook.com)

Alexander John Ellis

Rules and Regulations in Prisons in Ireland

PRISON RULES (IRELAND).

RETURN to an Order of the Honourable The House of Commons, dated 5t July 1888 ;—*for*,

COPY

OF

RULES AND REGULATIONS

IN FORCE IN THE

PRISONS IN IRELAND.

(*Mr. John Ellis.*)

Ordered, by The House of Commons, to be Printed,
7 *August* 1888.

LONDON:
PRINTED BY HENRY HANSARD AND SON;
AND
Published by EYRE and SPOTTISWOODE, East Harding-street, London, E.C.,
and 32, Abingdon-street, Westminster, S.W.;
ADAM and CHARLES BLACK, North Bridge, Edinburgh;
and HODGES, FIGGIS, and Co., 104, Grafton-street, Dublin.

CONTENTS.

LOCAL PRISONS.

RULES for LOCAL PRISONS, *Ireland*, approved by the LORD LIEUTENANT and PRIVY COUNCIL.

CONTENTS:

THE VISITING COMMITTEE.

By the Lord Lieutenant and Privy Council of Ireland.

Marlborough.

In pursuance of the General Prisons (Ireland) Act, 1877, We, John Winston, Duke of Marlborough, Lord Lieutenant General and General Governor of Ireland, by and with the advice, consent, and approval of the Privy Council of Ireland, have settled and do hereby approve the following rules with respect to the duties of each and every Visiting Committee appointed under the said Act.

Dated this 22nd day of March 1878.

Given at the Council Chamber in Dublin Castle.

(signed)   J. T. Ball, C.
Walter Crofton.
J. Michel, General.
Edward Gibson.

By the Lord Lieutenant General and General Governor of Ireland.

Marlborough.

In pursuance of the General Prisons (Ireland) Act, 1877, We, John Winston, Duke of Marlborough, Lord Lieutenant General and General Governor of Ireland, do hereby make and publish the following rules with respect to the duties of Visiting Committees.

1. The following rules shall apply to every Visiting Committee which, from and after the 1st day of April 1878, shall be appointed under the provisions of the 34th Section of the General Prisons (Ireland) Act, 1877.

2. The members of each Committee shall, from time to time and at frequent intervals, visit every prison for which they are appointed, and hear any complaints which may be made to them by the prisoners, and, if asked, shall do so privately.

3. The Visiting Committee shall report on any abuses within the prison, and also on any repairs which may be urgently required in the prison, and shall further take cognizance of any matters of pressing necessity and within the powers of their Commission as Justices, and shall do such acts and perform such duties in relation to the prison as they may be required to do or perform by any of these rules or by the Lord Lieutenant.

4. The

4. The Visiting Committee may exercise any powers vested at the time of the passing of the said Act in the Justices, or any one or more of them being members of a Board of Superintendence under the Prisons Act with respect to the punishment of prisoners. Every member of the Visiting Committee may visit the prison at any time, and shall at all times have free access to every part of the prison, and to every prisoner confined therein.

5. The Visiting Committee shall report to the Lord Lieutenant any matters with respect to which they may consider it expedient and shall report to the Lord Lieutenant, as soon as may be, and in such manner as is by these rules prescribed, or as he may direct, any matters respecting which they may be required by these rules or by him to report.

6. The Visiting Committee shall at their first meeting appoint a Chairman and make rules as regards their attendance at the prison for the purpose of carrying out the duties assigned to them.

7. The Chairman of the Visiting Committee shall report to the Lord Lieutenant the names and addresses of the members of the Visiting Committee.

8. No member of the Visiting Committee shall have any interest in any contract made in respect of any prison of which he is on the Visiting Committee.

9. The members of the Visiting Committee shall be treated with the utmost respect and courtesy by every prison officer. Any infringement of this rule will render the offender liable to severe punishment.

10. The Visiting Committee shall co-operate with the General Prisons Board in promoting the efficiency of the service, and shall make inquiry into any matter specially referred to them by the Lord Lieutenant or by the General Prisons Board, and report their opinion thereon.

11. Should any abuses in connection with the prison come to the knowledge of the Visiting Committee, or any of them, they shall take care that such abuses are brought to the notice of the General Prisons Board immediately, and in case of urgent necessity they may suspend any officer of the prison until the decision of the General Prisons Board is made known.

12. The Visiting Committee shall keep a book of minutes of their proceedings, in which all minutes shall be recorded.

13. The Visiting Committee shall hear and adjudicate on any report made by the Governor of the misconduct or idleness of any prisoner.

14. The Visiting Committee shall furnish such information with respect to the offences reported to them and the punishments they award, as may from time to time be required.

15. The Visiting Committee shall hear any complaint which any prisoner may desire to make to them; and, if necessary, report the same, with their opinion, to the General Prisons Board, or take such steps with regard to the matter as they may from time to time be directed to take.

16. The Visiting Committee shall attend to any report in writing which they may receive as to the mind or body of any prisoner being likely to be injured by the discipline or treatment to which he is subjected, and shall communicate their opinion to the General Prisons Board; if the case be urgent, they shall give such directions thereon as they may deem expedient, communicating the same to the General Prisons Board.

17. The Visiting Committee shall frequently inspect the diets of the prisoners, and if they shall find that the quality of any article does not fulfil the terms of the contract, they shall report the circumstances to the General Prisons Board, and note the same in their minute book, and the Governor shall thereupon take such steps as may be immediately necessary to provide the prisoners with suitable food.

18. The Visiting Committee may inspect any of the books of the prison.

19. The Visiting Committee shall report to the Lord Lieutenant any matter with respect to which they may consider it expedient.

20. The Visiting Committee may, on application from any non-criminal prisoner, dispense with his attendance at Divine Service on Sundays and other days.

21. The Visiting Committee, before granting any permission which, by the following rules, they are authorised or required to grant, shall satisfy themselves that it can be granted without interfering with the security, good order, and government of the prison and prisoners therein, and if after it has been granted its continuance seems likely to cause any such interference, or the prisoner has abused such permission, or has been guilty of any misconduct, they shall have power to suspend or withdraw such permission.

22. The

23. The Visiting Committee shall, on the application of any prisoner awaiting trial, if, having regard to his ordinary habits and condition of life, they think such special provision should be made in respect to him, permit any such prisoner—

(1.) To occupy, on payment of a small sum fixed by the General Prisons Board, a suitable room or cell specially fitted for such prisoners, and furnished with suitable bedding and other articles in addition to or different from those furnished for ordinary cells.

(2.) To exercise separately or with selected untried prisoners if the arrangements and construction of the prison permit it.

(3.) To have, at his own cost, the use of private furniture and utensils suitable to his ordinary habits, to be approved by the Governor.

(4.) To have, on payment of a small sum fixed by the General Prisons Board, the assistance of some person to be appointed by the Governor, relieving him from the performance of any unaccustomed tasks or offices.

23. The Visiting Committee may also permit the Governor to modify the routine of the prison in regard to any prisoner awaiting trial so far as to dispense with any practice which is, in the opinion of the Governor, clearly unnecessary in the case of that particular prisoner.

24. The Visiting Committee shall permit prisoners awaiting trial and misdemeanants of the first division to have supplied to them, at their own expense, such books, newspapers, or other means of occupation, other than those furnished by the prison, as are not, in their opinion, or in their absence pending their approval, in the opinion of the Governor, of an objectionable kind.

25. The Visiting Committee shall, on the application of any misdemeanant of the first division, permit him to wear his own clothing, provided that it is sufficient and is fit for use, and to supply his own food under the restrictions made in respect thereto; also if, having regard to his ordinary habits and condition of life, they think such special provision should be made in respect to him, they shall permit any such prisoner—

(1.) To occupy, on payment of a small sum fixed by the General Prisons Board, a room or cell specially fitted for such prisoners, and furnished with suitable bedding and other articles in addition to or different from those furnished for ordinary cells.

(2.) To have, at his own cost, the use of private furniture and utensils suitable to his ordinary habits, to be approved by the Governor.

(3.) To have, on payment of a small sum fixed by the General Prisons Board, the assistance of some person, to be appointed by the Governor, relieving him from the performance of any unaccustomed tasks or offices.

26. The Visiting Committee may, by permission, prolong the period of the visit allowed to any prisoner in any special case for special reasons. Further, they may, for special reasons in each case, permit any prisoner to have an extension of the privilege of communicating with his friends, either by visit or writing, provided such extension is in conformity with the rules relating to the class to which the prisoner belongs.

27. A person shall not, without an order from a member of the Visiting Committee, be permitted to visit a prisoner under order for execution, except as authorised by the rules in force at the time; and if such prisoner applies to the Governor to be allowed to be visited by any person, the name of such person shall be forthwith submitted to the Visiting Committee.

28. If the Visiting Committee shall, on the application of any prisoner, be satisfied that on his admission he made a mis-statement of his religion, they may allow him to be recorded as of the religion to which it may be proved to their satisfaction that he in fact belonged.

29. The Visiting Committee are requested to give such assistance as may be in their power towards securing the proper disposal of any prisoner which may be earned by prisoners, especially in places where there is no Discharged Prisoners' Aid Society, according to such instructions as may from time to time be issued.

30. The Visiting Committee shall also discharge such other duties as are assigned to them in the special rules for the time being in force with respect to special classes of prisoners, and in the General Rules for the time being in force for the government of prisons.

31. The foregoing rules shall come into operation upon the expiration of 40 days after the same shall have been laid before Parliament.

Made and published this 22nd day of March 1878.

SPECIAL RULES FOR PRISONERS AWAITING TRIAL.

By the General Prisons Board for Ireland.

In pursuance of the General Prisons (Ireland) Act, 1877, the General Prisons Board for Ireland hereby make the following Special Rules with respect to Prisoners awaiting Trial.

Admission, Discharge, and Removal.

1. Such prisoner shall not be required to take a bath on reception, if on the application of the prisoner the Governor shall decide that it is unnecessary, or the Surgeon shall state that it is for medical reasons unadvisable.

2. In order to prevent such prisoners from being contaminated by each other, or endeavouring to defeat the ends of justice, they shall be kept separate, and shall not be permitted to communicate together.

3. Such prisoners while attending chapel, and at other times shall, if possible, be placed so that they may not be in view of the convicted prisoners.

4. The Visiting Committee or Governor, before granting any permission which, by the following rules, they are authorised or required to grant, shall satisfy themselves that it can be granted without interfering with the security, good order, and government of the prison and prisoners therein; and if after it has been granted its continuance seems likely to cause any such interference, or the prisoner has abused such permission or been guilty of any misconduct, the Visiting Committee shall have power to suspend and withdraw such permission, and in the like circumstances the Governor may suspend or withdraw the same if it has been granted by himself, or suspend it when it has been granted by the Visiting Committee if the case be urgent, provided that he report the case within twenty-four hours to them.*

5. The Visiting Committee shall, on the application of any such prisoner, if, having regard to his ordinary habits and condition of life, they think such special provisions should be made in respect of him, permit any such prisoner—

    (1.) To occupy, on payment of a small sum fixed by the General Prisons Board, a suitable room or cell specially fitted for such prisoner, and furnished with suitable bedding and other articles in addition to or different from those furnished for ordinary cells.

    (2.) To exercise separately or with selected untried prisoners, if the arrangements and construction of the prison permit it.

    (3.) To have at his own cost the use of private furniture and utensils suitable to his ordinary habits, to be approved by the Governor.

    (4.) To have on payment of a small sum fixed by the General Prisons Board, the assistance of some person to be appointed by the Governor, relieving him from the performance of any unaccustomed task or office.

6. Any money in the hands of the Governor belonging to any such prisoner may be applied to the purpose of making special provision for him in cases where the prisoner is, by these rules, required to make any payment in respect of such special provision.

7. The Visiting Committee may also permit the Governor to modify the routine of the prison in regard to any such prisoner so far as to dispense with any practice which in the opinion of the Governor is clearly unnecessary in the case of that particular prisoner.

8. The Governor shall, on the application of any such prisoner, permit him to have any books, papers, or documents such as are referred to in Section 15 of the General Prisons (Ireland) Act, 1877, 40 & 41 Vict., c. 49.

Food, Clothing, and Bedding.

9. Any such prisoner who prefers to provide his own food for any meal shall give notice thereof beforehand at the time required, but the Governor shall not permit any such prisoner to receive any prison allowance of food for the meal for which he procures or receives food at his own expense.

10. Articles

---

* See further Special Rules for prisoners awaiting trial, pp. 24, 25.

10. Articles of food shall be received only at such hours as may be laid down from time to time. They shall be inspected by the officers of the prison, and shall be subject to such restrictions as may be necessary to prevent luxury or waste.

11. Any such prisoner shall not during the 24 hours receive or purchase more than one pint of beer, cider, or other fermented liquor, or (if an adult) half-a-pint (8 ozs.) of wine.

12. No such prisoner shall be allowed to sell or transfer any article whatsoever allowed to be introduced for his use to any other person.

Personal Cleanliness.

13. Such prisoner shall not be compelled either to have his hair cut or (if he usually wears his beard, &c.) to shave, except on request of vermin or dirt, or when the Surgeon deems it necessary on the ground of health and cleanliness, and the hair of such prisoner shall not be cut closer than may be necessary for the purpose of health and cleanliness.

14. The beds of such prisoners shall be made, and the rooms and yards in their occupation shall be swept and cleaned every morning. The furniture and utensils appropriated to their use shall be kept clean and neatly arranged. Should any such prisoner object to perform any of these duties, they may be performed for him, as provided in Rule 6, Sub-section 4.

Health of Prisoners.

15. If any such prisoner who is out of health shall desire the attendance of his usual medical man, the Visiting Committee may, if they are satisfied that the application is bonâ fide, permit him to be visited by such medical man at his own expense, and to be supplied with medicine by him, proper precautions being in all cases observed to prevent abuse of these privileges.

Instruction.

16. Such prisoner may be permitted to have supplied to him, at his own expense, such books,* newspapers, or other means of occupation, other than those furnished by the prison, as are not, in the opinion of the Visiting Committee, or in their absence and pending their approval, in the opinion of the Governor, of an objectionable kind.

Visits to and Communication with Prisoners.

17. So far as prison arrangements may admit facilities shall be given to such prisoners to work and follow their respective trades and employments, and all earnings of such prisoner, after payment thereof of such sum as the General Prison Board may determine on account of the cost of his maintenance in the prison, or on account of the use of implements lent to him, shall belong to such prisoner.

18. Each such prisoner shall be permitted to be visited by one person, or (if circumstances permit) by two persons at the same time, for a quarter of an hour on any week-day, during such hours as may from time to time be appointed.†

19. The Visiting Committee may, by permission in any special case for special reasons, prolong the period of the visit allowed to any such prisoner, or allow him to be visited by more than two persons at the same time.

20. Every endeavour shall be made to provide that such prisoners shall not, when being visited, be exposed to the view of the friends of other prisoners, and to prevent the friends of one prisoner from coming in contact with the friends of another while in the prison.

21. Such prisoner shall at his request be allowed to see his legal adviser (by which is to be understood a certificated solicitor or his clerk, if such clerk is furnished by his principal with written authority) on any week-day at any reasonable hour, and, if required, in private (but, if necessary, in the view of an officer of the prison).

22. Any such prisoner who is in prison in default of bail shall be permitted to see any of his friends, on any week-day, at any reasonable hour, for the bonâ fide purpose of providing bail.

23. Paper

* See Rule 1, p. 14.   † See Rule, p. 64.

A 4

23. Paper and all other writing materials to such extent as may appear reasonable to the Governor shall be furnished to any such prisoner who requires to be so supplied for the purposes of communicating with friends, or preparing a defence. Any confidential written communication prepared as instructions for a solicitor may be delivered personally to him or his authorised clerk, without being previously examined by any officer of the prison; but all other written communications are to be examined as letters, and are not to be sent out of the prison without being previously inspected by the Governor.

24. The foregoing rules relating to prisoners awaiting trial shall apply to any person committed to prison for safe custody in any of the following circumstances:—

(a.) On his commitment for trial for any indictable offence.

(b.) Pending the preliminary hearing before justices of a charge against him of an indictable offence, or pending the hearing of an information or complaint against him.

(c.) On default in entering into recognizances or finding surety or sureties.

25. Prisoners before trial may, if they desire it, wear the prison dress, and they shall be required to do so if their own clothes are insufficient or unfit for use, or necessary to be preserved for the purposes of justice. The prison dress for prisoners before trial shall be different from that of the convicted prisoners.

26. Prisoners awaiting trial shall also be subject to any general rules for the time being in force for the government of prisons, except so far as the same are inconsistent with the special rules relating to such prisoners.*

27. The foregoing rules shall apply to every ordinary prison and shall come into operation upon the expiration of 60 days after the same, having been settled and approved by the Lord Lieutenant and Privy Council, shall have been laid before Parliament.

Made and executed this 22nd day of March 1878, by "The General Prisons Board for Ireland."

Walter Crofton, Chairman.

By the Lord Lieutenant and Privy Council of Ireland.

Marlborough.

In pursuance of the General Prisons (Ireland) Act, 1877, We, John Winston, Duke of Marlborough, Lord Lieutenant General and General Governor of Ireland, with the approval, advice, and consent of the Privy Council of Ireland, have settled, and hereby approve of the foregoing special rules with respect to prisoners awaiting trial, made by the General Prisons Board for Ireland.

Dated this 22nd day of March 1878.

Given at the Council Chamber in Dublin Castle.

J. T. Ball, C.
Walter Crofton.
J. Nickel, General.
Edward Gibson.

SPECIAL RULES FOR MISDEMEANANTS OF FIRST DIVISION.

By the General Prisons Board for Ireland.

In pursuance of the General Prisons (Ireland) Act, 1877, the General Prisons Board for Ireland hereby make the following Special Rules with respect to prisoners who are misdemeanants of the first division.

Admission, Discharge, and Removal.

1. No person shall be placed in this division except as provided by statute, or by order of the Judge or court before whom he is tried.

2. Such prisoner shall not be required to take a bath on reception, if on the application of the prisoner the Governor shall decide that it is unnecessary, or the Surgeon shall state that it is, for medical reasons, unadvisable.

S. Every

3. Every such prisoner shall be searched only by an officer specially appointed for the purpose.

4. He shall be placed as soon as possible after reception in a cell appropriated to prisoners of his class, unless there is reason to believe that he is suffering from some infectious disease, in which case he shall be detained in a reception cell till he can be seen by the Surgeon.

5. He shall at all times, except when at chapel or exercise, occupy the room or cell assigned to him.

6. He shall not be placed in association or at exercise with criminal prisoners.

7. The Visiting Committee or Governor, before granting any permission which, by the following rules, they are authorised or required to grant, shall satisfy themselves that it can be granted without interfering with the security, good order, and government of the prison and prisoners therein, and if after it has been granted, its continuance seems likely to cause any such interference, or the prisoner has abused such permission, or been guilty of any misconduct, the Visiting Committee shall have power to suspend and withdraw such permission, and in the like circumstances, the Governor may suspend or withdraw the same if it has been granted by himself, or suspend it when it has been granted by the Visiting Committee, if the case is urgent, provided that he report the same within 24 hours to them.

8. The Visiting Committee shall, on the application of any such prisoner, if, having regard to his ordinary habits and conditions of life, they think such special provision should be made in respect to him, permit any such prisoner:—

(1.) To occupy, on payment of a small sum fixed by the General Prisons Board, a room or cell specially fitted for such prisoners, and furnished with suitable bedding and other articles in addition to or different from those furnished for ordinary cells.

(2.) To have, at his own cost, the use of private furniture and utensils suitable to his ordinary habits, to be approved by the Governor.

(3.) To have, on payment of a small sum, to be fixed by the General Prisons Board, the assistance of some person to be appointed by the Governor, relieving him from the performance of any non-occupational tasks or offices.

9. Any money in the hands of the Governor, belonging to any such prisoner, may be applied to the purpose of making special provision for him, in cases where the prisoner is by these rules required to make any payment in respect of such special provision.

Food, Clothing, and Bedding of Prisoners.

10. He shall be permitted by the Visiting Committee to supply his own food on giving due notice beforehand, at the time required; but the Governor shall not permit such prisoner to receive any prison allowance of food at any meal for which he procures or receives food at his own expense.

11. Articles of food shall be received only at such hours as may be laid down from time to time. They shall be inspected by the officers of the prison, and shall be subject to such restrictions as may be necessary to prevent luxury or waste.

12. Any such person shall not, during the 24 hours, receive or purchase more than one pint of beer, cider, or other fermented liquor, or (if an adult), half a pint (8 ozs.) of wine.

13. He shall be permitted by the Visiting Committee to wear his own clothing, provided that it is sufficient and is fit for use.

14. No such prisoner shall be allowed to sell or transfer any article whatsoever allowed to be introduced for his use to any other person.

Personal Cleanliness.

15. Such prisoner shall not be compelled either to have his hair cut or (if he usually wears his beard, &c.) to shave, except on account of vermin or dirt, or when the Surgeon deems it necessary on the ground of health and cleanliness; and the hair of such prisoner shall not be cut closer than may be necessary for the purpose of health and cleanliness.

16. The beds of such prisoners shall be made, and the room and yards in their occupation shall be swept and cleaned every morning. The furniture and utensils appropriated to their use shall be kept clean and neatly arranged. Should any such prisoner object to perform any of these duties they may be performed for him as provided in Rule 8, Sub-section 3.

17. Such

Instruction.

17. Each prisoner may be permitted to have supplied to him at his own expense such books, newspapers, or other means of occupation, other than those furnished by the prison, as are not in the opinion of the Visiting Committee, or, in their absence, and pending their approval, in the opinion of the Governor, of an objectionable kind.

Employment.

18. Such prisoners may be permitted to work and may follow their respective trades and professions. Such prisoners as find their own implements, and are not maintained at the expense of the prison, shall be allowed to receive the whole of their earnings ; but the earnings of such as are furnished with implements, or are maintained at the expense of the prison, shall be subject to a deduction to be determined by the General Prisons Board for the use of implements and the cost of maintenance.

Visits to and Communications with Prisoners.

19. The Visiting Committee may, by permission in any special case, for special reasons, prolong the period of the visit allowed to any such prisoner, or accord additional visits or letters to such reasonable extent as they may deem advisable.

20. The place in which such prisoners receive their visits shall not be the same as that in which criminal prisoners receive their visits, if any other suitable place can conveniently be provided.

21. No other privileges than the foregoing shall be allowed to such prisoners.

22. The foregoing regulations relating to misdemeanants of the first division shall (to the exclusion of any other regulations applicable exclusively to any particular class of prisoners) apply also to—

(a.) Any prisoner committed under any rule, order, or attachment for contempt of court.

(b.) Any prisoner sentenced to imprisonment on conviction for sedition or seditious libel.

23. Misdemeanants of the first division shall also be subject to any general rules for the time being in force for the government of prisons, except so far as the same are inconsistent with the special rules relating to such misdemeanants.

24. The foregoing rules shall apply to every ordinary prison, and shall come into operation upon the expiration of 40 days after the same, having been settled and approved by the Lord Lieutenant and Privy Council, shall have been laid before Parliament.

Made and executed this 22nd day of March 1878, by " The General Prisons Board for Ireland."

Walter Crofton, Chairman.

By the Lord Lieutenant and Privy Council of Ireland.

Marlborough.

In pursuance of the General Prisons (Ireland) Act, 1877, We, John Winston, Duke of Marlborough, Lord Lieutenant General and General Governor of Ireland with the approval, advice, and consent of the Privy Council of Ireland, have settled, and hereby approve of the foregoing Special Rules with respect to Prisoners who are Misdemeanants of the First Division, made by the General Prisons Board for Ireland.

Dated this 22nd day of March 1878.

Given at the Council Chamber in Dublin Castle.

J. T. Ball, C.
Walter Crofton.
J. Michel, Genl.
Edward Gibson.

SPECIAL RULES FOR DEBTORS.

By the General Prison Board for Ireland.

In pursuance of the General Prison (Ireland) Act, 1877, the General Prison Board for Ireland hereby make the following Special Rules with respect to prisoners who are debtors.

Admission, Discharge, and Removal.

1. Such prisoner shall not be required to take a bath on reception, if on the application of the prisoner the Governor shall decide that it is unnecessary, or the Surgeon shall state that it is, for medical reasons, unadvisable.

2. He shall at all times, except when at chapel or exercise, occupy the cell or room assigned to him.

Food, Clothing, and Bedding.

3. Any such prisoner who prefers to provide his own food shall give notice thereof beforehand at the time required, but the Governor shall not permit such prisoner to receive any prison allowance of food on any day whereon he procures or receives food at his own expense.

4. Articles of food shall be received only at such hours as may be laid down from time to time. They shall be inspected by the officers of the prison, and shall be subject to such restrictions as may be necessary to prevent luxury or waste.

5. Any such prisoner shall not, during the 24 hours, receive or purchase more than one pint of beer, cider, or other fermented liquor, or (if an adult) half-a-pint (8 oz.) of wine.

6. No such prisoner shall be allowed to sell or transfer any article whatsoever allowed to be introduced for his use to any other person.

Personal Cleanliness.

7. Such prisoner shall not be compelled either to have his hair cut, or (if he usually wears his beard, &c.) to shave, except on account of vermin or dirt, or when the Surgeon deems it necessary on the ground of health and cleanliness, and the hair of such prisoner shall not be cut closer than may be necessary for the purpose of health and cleanliness.

8. The beds of such prisoners shall be made and the rooms and yards in their occupation shall be swept and cleaned by them every morning. The furniture and utensils appropriated to their use shall be kept clean and neatly arranged by them.

Visits to and Communications with Prisoners.

9. The Visiting Committee or Governor before granting any permission which by the following rules they are authorised or required to grant, shall satisfy themselves that it can be granted without interfering with the security, good order, and government of the prison and prisoners therein, and if, after it has been granted, its continuance seems likely to cause any interference, or the prisoner has abused such permission, or been guilty of any mis-conduct, the Visiting Committee shall have power to suspend and withdraw such permission, and in the like circumstances the Governor may suspend or withdraw the same if it has been granted by himself, or, if the case is urgent, suspend it if it has been granted by the Visiting Committee, provided that he report the same within 24 hours to them.

10. The place in which such prisoners receive their visits shall not be the same as that in which criminal prisoners receive their visits, if any other suitable place can conveniently be provided.

11. Each such prisoner shall be permitted to be visited by one friend or relation, or (if circumstances permit) by two such persons at the same time once a month for a period of a quarter of an hour, during such hours as may from time to time be appointed. They shall also be allowed to write one letter and to receive one letter in each month.

12. The

12. The Visiting Committee may, by permission in any special case, for special reasons prolong the period of the visit allowed to any such prisoner, or allow him to be visited by more than two persons at the same time.

13. Debtors shall also be subject to any general rules for the time being in force for the government of Prisons, except so far as the same are inconsistent with the special rules relating to debtors.

14. The foregoing rules relating to debtors shall apply to any person committed to prison for default in payment of any debt, or instalment of any debt due from such person in pursuance of any order or judgment of any county court or other competent court, or any order of a justice or justices, unless, by the terms of the warrant of commitment, the imprisonment is to be with hard labour, or is in default of payment of a penal sum.

15. The foregoing rules shall apply to every ordinary prison, and shall come into operation upon the expiration of 40 days after the same, having been settled and approved by the Lord Lieutenant and Privy Council, shall have been laid before Parliament.

Made and executed this 22nd day of March 1878, by "The General Prisons Board for Ireland."

(signed) *Walter Crofton*, Chairman.

By the Lord Lieutenant and Privy Council of Ireland.

Marlborough.

In pursuance of the General Prisons (Ireland) Act, 1877, We, John Winston, Duke of Marlborough, Lord Lieutenant General and General Governor of Ireland, with the approval, advice, and consent of the Privy Council of Ireland, have settled, and hereby approve of the foregoing Special Rules with respect to Prisoners who are Debtors, made by the General Prisons Board for Ireland.

Dated this 22nd day of March 1878.

Given at the Council Chamber in Dublin Castle.

J. T. Ball, C.
Walter Crofton.
J. Michel, (Lieut.
Edward Gibson.

GENERAL RULES FOR PRISONERS.

By the General Prisons Board for Ireland.

In pursuance of the General Prisons (Ireland) Act, 1877, the General Prisons Board for Ireland hereby make the following General Rules for the government of Prisons.

General.

1. The walls and ceilings of the wards, cells, rooms, and passages used by the prisoners throughout every prison shall be scraped and limewashed, at least twice in the year; and the day room, passages, and sleeping cells shall be washed or cleaned once a week, or oftener, if requisite; the straw shall be changed once in every two months; convenient places for the prisoners to wash themselves shall be provided, with an adequate allowance of soap, towels, and combs.

2. Nothing shall be allowed to grow against the outer walls of the prison, nor any rubbish or other articles to be laid against them, nor shall any tools or implements of any kind likely to facilitate escape be left unnecessarily exposed.

3. Thermometers shall be placed in different parts of the prison.

4. No person shall be permitted to sleep in the apartments of any officer of the prison without permission from the Governor, each permission to be reported to the Visiting Committee.

5. A report

5. A report shall be made to the Governor at ten o'clock each night whether the officers resident in the prison are all present, and no ingress or egress shall be allowed into or out of the prison between the hours of ten o'clock at night and six o'clock in the morning, except to the Governor and his family, the Chaplain, or Surgeon, or in special cases, which shall be entered in the journal of the Governor.

Hours of locking and unlocking the prison.

Admission and Discharge of Prisoners.

6. Prisoners, unless they are exempted by the medical officer, shall go into a bath on admission before being passed to their proper wards, and subsequently once every fortnight or oftener if necessary; but no prisoner shall be stripped or bathed in the presence of any other prisoner.

Bath.

7. Prisoners on admission shall be searched, and all dangerous weapons, articles calculated to facilitate escape, and prohibited articles, shall be taken from them.

Search of prisoners on admission.

8. No prisoner shall be searched by any other prisoner.

Prisoner to be searched.

9. All money or other effects brought into the prison by any prisoner or sent to the prison, for his use, which he is not allowed to retain, shall be placed in the custody of the Governor, who shall keep an inventory of them in a separate book.

Effects retained by Governor.

10. The name, age, religious denomination, height, weight, features, particular marks, and general appearance of a prisoner shall, upon his admission, be noted in a nominal record of prisoners, to be kept by the Governor. Every prisoner shall also, as soon as possible, be examined by the Surgeon, who shall enter in a book to be kept by the Governor a record of the state of health of the prisoner, and any observations he may deem it expedient to add.

Register of certain particulars relating to prisoners.

11. All prisoners, previously to being removed to any other prison, or being discharged from prison, shall be examined by the Surgeon; and no prisoner shall be removed to any other prison unless the Surgeon certifies, by an entry in the nominal record, that the prisoner is free from any illness that renders him unfit for removal, and no prisoner shall be discharged from prison if labouring under an attack or dangerous distemper, or until, in the opinion of the Surgeon, such discharge is safe, unless such prisoner require to be discharged.

Removal and discharge of prisoners.

12. Before a prisoner under the age of 16 years be discharged, his or her relatives and friends shall be informed on what day and at what time he or she will be discharged.

Discharge of prisoners.

13. Prisoners before trial shall be kept apart from convicted prisoners.

Separation of prisoners.

14. Every prisoner may, if required for purposes of justice, be photographed on reception and subsequently; but no copy of such photograph shall be given to any person except those officially authorised to receive it for the purposes of identification.

Photography.

15. Female prisoners shall be searched on admission by female officers. In other respects the same course shall be pursued in reference to the admission, removal, or discharge of a female prisoner as in the case of a male prisoner, the Matron performing the duties imposed in the case of a male prisoner on the Governor.

Female prisoners and their children.

16. The child of a female prisoner may be received into prison with its mother provided it is at the breast; in all such cases an authority from the committing magistrate for the child's admission should accompany the prisoner on reception.

17. Any such child so admitted shall not be taken from its mother until the Surgeon of the prison certifies that it is in a condition to be removed.

18. When any such child has attained the age of nine months the Surgeon shall report whether it is desirable or necessary that it should be any longer retained, but except under special circumstances no such child shall be kept in prison after it has arrived at the age of 12 months.

19. Any such child so retained may be supplied with clothing at the public expense.

20. Previous to the discharge of any such child the Governor shall ascertain from the relations whether they are willing and in a position to receive it; in the event of their being unable to do so, he shall cause it to be sent to the workhouse of the union in which the mother was apprehended, having previously communicated with the workhouse authorities.

Food, Clothing, and Bedding of Prisoners.

21. No tap shall be kept in any prison; nor shall spirituous liquors of any kind be admitted for the use of any of the prisoners therein under any pretence whatever, unless by a written order of the Surgeon, specifying the quantity and for whom; no wine, beer, cider, or other fermented liquors shall be admitted for the use of any prisoners

Spirituous liquors.

except in such quantities, in such manner, and at such times as shall be allowed by the rules.

Smoking.   22. No smoking shall be allowed, or tobacco introduced, except with the consent and subject to any restrictions prescribed by the General Prisons Board, or under a written order of the Surgeon.

Order of Surgeon as to spirituous liquors, &c.   23. Any order of the Surgeon for the admission to prisoners of spirituous liquors or tobacco shall be entered by him in his journal, stating the quantity allowed on each occasion.

Plank bed.   24. A convicted criminal prisoner shall, during the whole of his sentence, when it does not exceed one month, and during one month of his sentence when it exceeds one month, be required to sleep on a plank bed. The prisoner shall be allowed the opportunity of earning by industry the gradual remission of this requirement after the expiration of one month; but after he has earned such remission he shall be liable to forfeit the same on account of idleness, inattention to instruction, or misconduct.*

Clean linen.   25. Every prisoner shall be supplied with clean linen at least once in every week.

Prison allowance of food for convicted prisoner.   26. Every convicted criminal prisoner shall be allowed a sufficient quantity of food according to the scale sanctioned by the Lord Lieutenant. Prisoners under the care of the Surgeon shall be allowed such diet as he may direct. Care shall be taken that all provisions supplied to the prisoners be of proper quality and weight. Scales and legal weights and measures shall be provided, open to the use of any prisoners under such restrictions as may be prescribed by the General Prisons Board.

Convicted prisoner restricted to prison allowance.   27. No convicted criminal prisoner shall be allowed any wine, beer, or other fermented liquor, or shall receive any food, clothing, bedding, or necessaries other than the prison allowance, except under a written order from the Surgeon, to be entered in his journal, specifying the quantity, and the name of the prisoner for whom such article is intended; such orders to be immediately reported by the Governor to the Visiting Committee.

Dress of convicted criminal.   28. A convicted criminal prisoner shall be provided with a complete prison dress, and shall be required to wear it.

Return of clothing to discharged prisoner.   29. On the discharge of a prisoner his own clothes shall be returned to him unless it has been found necessary to destroy them, in which case he shall be provided with clothing.

Purification of clothing of prisoner.   30. If necessary, the clothes of the prisoner shall be purified before he is allowed to wear them in the prison or to take them on his discharge.

Bed.   31. Every male prisoner shall sleep in a cell by himself, or under special circumstances in a separate bed placed in a cell containing not fewer than two other male prisoners, and sufficient bed-clothes shall be provided for every prisoner. Epileptic prisoners or prisoners labouring under disease requiring assistance or supervision in the night, may at any time, notwithstanding this regulation, be placed by order of the Surgeon with not fewer than two other male prisoners.

Bedding.   32. The bed-clothes shall be aired, changed, and washed so often as the Surgeon or the General Prisons Board may direct.

Personal Cleanliness.

Personal cleanliness of prisoners.   33. Prisoners shall be required to keep themselves clean, and decent in their persons, and to conform to such rules as may be laid down for that purpose.

Washing.   34. Each prisoner shall wash himself thoroughly at least once every day; and the Governor shall see that there is a sufficient supply of soap, towels, and combs for such purpose.

Shaving.   35. Each male prisoner shall have his beard clipped, or be shaved at least once a week unless specially exempted by the Governor or Surgeon.

Hair cutting.   36. The hair of a female prisoner shall not be cut without her consent, except on account of vermin or dirt, or when the Surgeon deems it requisite on the ground of health, and the hair of male criminal prisoners shall not be cut closer than may be necessary for purposes of health and cleanliness.

Employment of Prisoners.

Prohibition of gaming.   37. No gaming shall be permitted in any prison, and the Governor shall seize and destroy all dice, cards, or other instruments of gaming.

38. A male

* See Rule No. 1, page 23.

38. A male prisoner above 16 years of age, who has been committed to prison to be imprisoned with hard labour shall, during the whole of his sentence, when it does not exceed one month, and during the first month of his sentence when it exceeds one month, be kept to penal labour, and he shall for the rest of his term of imprisonment be kept to industrial labour. Provided that any such prisoner who is not sufficiently industrious or is inattentive to instruction, or guilty of misconduct shall be liable. If at the time of the offence he is being subjected to penal labour, to be kept to such penal labour for a further period, or if at the time of the offence he is being subjected to industrial labour, to be put back again to penal labour.*

39. Every male prisoner under the age of 16 years sentenced to hard labour, and every female prisoner sentenced to hard labour, shall be kept at industrial labour during such number of hours not more than 10 or less than six (exclusive of meals) in each day, as may be prescribed by the General Prisons Board, unless the Surgeon certifies that he or she is unfit for hard labour.

40. No prisoner shall be employed in unnecessary labour on Sundays, Christmas Day, Good Friday, 1st and 6th January, 17th and 25th March, Ascension Day, the first Thursday after Trinity Sunday, the 29th June, the 15th August, and 1st of November, and days appointed for a general fast or thanksgiving.

41. Every prisoner sentenced to hard labour shall be examined by the Surgeon before being put to such labour, and he shall certify whether any such prisoner is unfit to be kept at labour of either class, and he shall from time to time examine the prisoners sentenced to hard labour during the time of their being so employed, and shall enter in his journal the name of any prisoner whom health he thinks to be endangered by a continuance at labour of either class, and thereupon each prisoner shall not again be employed at such class of labour until the Surgeon certifies that he is fit for such employment.

42. Each prisoner, before being put to tread-wheel labour, shall be examined by the Surgeon, and he shall report, for the Governor's information and guidance, whether any such prisoner is fit or otherwise for such labour.

43. Provision shall be made by the General Prisons Board for the employment of all convicted criminal prisoners not sentenced to hard labour. The General Prisons Board shall issue instructions as to the amount and nature of such employment, but no prisoner not sentenced to hard labour shall be punished for neglect of work, excepting by such alteration in the scale of diet as may be prescribed by the General Prisons Board in the case of neglect of work by such prisoners.

Health of Prisoners.

44. Criminal prisoners, if employed at work in their own cells, shall be permitted to take such exercise in the open air as the Surgeon may deem necessary for their health.

45. The names of the prisoners who desire to see the Surgeon, or appear out of health, shall be reported by the officer attending them to the Governor, and by him without delay to the Surgeon.

46. All directions given by the surgeon in relation to any prisoner, with the exception of orders for the supply of medicines or directions in relation to such matters as are carried into effect by the surgeon himself, or under his superintendence, shall be entered day by day in his journal, which shall have a separate column in which entries are to be made by the Governor, stating in respect of each direction the fact of its having been or not having been complied with, accompanied by such observations, if any, as the Governor may think fit to make, and the date of the entry.

47. In every prison an infirmary or proper place for the reception of sick prisoners shall be provided.

Religious Instruction.

48. One or more chapel or chapels, with separate divisions for males and females, shall be set apart for Divine Worship and the religious and moral instruction of the prisoners in every prison, and shall not be employed for any other purpose.

49. [Annulled. See Amended Rule, page 77.]

50. Except

* See Rule II., p. 12.
B 4

Books and printed papers. 50. Except as provided by special rules, no books or printed papers shall be admitted into any prison for the use of the prisoners, except by permission of the General Prisons Board; and no books or printed papers intended for the religious instruction of prisoners shall be admitted but those chosen by the chaplain of the persuasion to which the prisoner belongs: provided that in case there may be a difference of opinion between the Chaplain and the General Prisons Board with respect to books or papers proposed to be admitted for the religious instruction of a prisoner, reference shall be had to his bishop or constituted ecclesiastical authority, whose decision shall be final; and, subject to such permission of the General Prisons Board as aforesaid, all books or printed papers admitted into any prison for the religious instruction of prisoners belonging to any other persuasion, and who are visited by a minister of such persuasion, shall be approved by such minister; and the Governor shall keep a catalogue of all books and printed papers admitted into the prison.

51. All prisoners who, in the opinion of the surgeon, are in danger of death, shall be permitted to receive the attendance and spiritual service of any minister of any religious persuasion whom they shall express a wish to see.

Instruction.

Instruction of prisoners. 52. Provision shall be made in every prison for the instruction of prisoners in reading, writing, and arithmetic during such hours and to such extent as the General Prisons Board may deem expedient, provided that such hours shall not be deducted from the hours prescribed for hard labour.

Visits to and Communications with Prisoners.

Power of Governor as to visitors. 53. The Governor may demand the name and address of any visitor to a prisoner; and when he has any ground for suspicion may search, or cause to be searched, male visitors, and may direct the matron or some other female officer to search female visitors, such search not to be in the presence of any prisoner or of another visitor; and in case of any visitor refusing to be searched, the Governor may deny him or her admission; the grounds of such proceeding, with the particulars thereof, to be entered in his journal.

Prison Offences.

General regulations as to punishment. 54. No prisoner shall be punished until he has had an opportunity of hearing the charges and evidence against him, and of making his defence.

Punishment diet by Visiting Committee. 55. A prisoner may be punished by the Visiting Committee by placing such prisoner on punishment diet, according to the prescribed scale, for any period not exceeding 28 days, as well as by the withdrawal of any privilege granted by special permission or otherwise in accordance with the rules.

Punishment diet by Governor. 56. A prisoner may be punished by the Governor by placing such prisoner on punishment diet according to the prescribed scale for any period not exceeding three days, as well as by withdrawal of any privilege granted by special permission or otherwise in accordance with the rules.

57. No punishment or privations of any kind shall be awarded, except by the General Prisons Board, the Visiting Committee, the Inspector, or the Governor, or by other duly authorised persons.

Governor to punish for prison offences. 58. The Governor shall have power to hear complaints respecting any of the offences following; that is to say,—

1. Disobedience of the regulations of the prison by any prisoner.
2. Common assaults by one prisoner on another;
3. Profane cursing and swearing by any prisoner;
4. Indecent behaviour by any prisoner;
5. Irreverent behaviour at chapel by any prisoner;
6. Insulting or threatening language by any prisoner to any officer or prisoner;
7. Absence from chapel without leave by any criminal prisoner;
8. Idleness or negligence at work by any criminal prisoner;
9. Wilful mismanagement of work by any criminal prisoner;

All the above acts are declared to be offences against prison discipline; and it shall be lawful for the Governor to examine any person committing such offence, and to determine thereupon, and to punish such offence by ordering any offender, for any time not exceeding 24 hours, to close confinement, to be kept there upon bread and water. And the

the Governor shall enter in a separate book called the Punishment Book a statement of the nature of any offence that he has punished in pursuance of this regulation, with the addition of the name of the offender, the date of the offence, and the amount of punishment inflicted.

59. If any criminal prisoner is guilty of repeated offences against prison discipline, or is guilty of any offence which the Governor is not empowered to punish, the Governor shall report the same to the Visiting Committee, or one of them; and any one of such Committee, or any other Justice having jurisdiction in the place in which the prison belongs, or a member of the General Prisons Board, shall have power to inquire upon oath and to determine concerning any matter so reported to him, and to order the offender to be punished by confinement in a punishment cell for any term not exceeding 14 days. — *Punishment of prisoners by Visiting Committee.*

60. No prisoner shall be put in irons or under mechanical restraint by the Governor of any prison except in case of urgent necessity; and the particulars of every such case shall be forthwith entered in the Governor's journal, and notice forthwith given thereof to the General Prisons Board; and no prisoner shall be kept in irons, or under mechanical restraint excepting as provided by the 17th Rule, 30th sec., 7 Geo. 4, cap. 74.† — *Use of irons.*

61. [Annulled. *See* Amended General Rule, No. 1, page 63.]

Prisoners under Sentence of Death.

62. Every prisoner under warrant or order for execution shall, immediately on his arrival in the prison after sentence, be searched by, or by the orders of the Governor, and all articles shall be taken from him which the Governor deems it dangerous or inexpedient to leave in his possession. He shall be confined in a cell apart from all other prisoners, and shall be placed by day and by night under the constant charge of an officer. He shall be allowed such dietary and amount of exercise as the Governor and Surgeon with the approval of the General Prisons Board may direct. The Chaplain shall have free access to every such prisoner of his own religious persuasion, and free access shall be allowed to any clergyman whom such prisoner desires to see. With the above exceptions, no person not being a member of the Visiting Committee, or an officer of the prison, shall have access to the prisoner, except in pursuance of an order from the Visiting Committee.

During the preparation for an execution, and the time of the execution, no person shall enter the prison who is not legally entitled to do so, unless in pursuance of an order in writing from two or more members of the Visiting Committee. — *Prisoners under sentence of death.*

THE GOVERNOR.

63. The Governor shall reside in the prison. He shall not be an Under Sheriff or Bailiff, or be concerned in any other employment. — *Residence of Governor.*

64. The Governor shall strictly conform to the law relating to prisons, and to the prison regulations, and shall be responsible for the due observance of them by others. If a shall observe the conduct of the prison officers, and enforce on each of them the due execution of his duties, and shall not permit any subordinate officer to be employed in any private capacity, either for any other officer of the prison, or for any prisoner. — *Governor to conform to law and regulations of Prison.*

65. The Governor shall, in case of misconduct, have power to suspend any subordinate officer, and shall report the particulars without delay to the General Prisons Board. — *May suspend subordinate officers.*

66. The Governor shall visit the whole of the prison, and see every male prisoner once at least in every 24 hours, and in default of such daily visits and inspections he shall state in his journal how far he has omitted them, and the cause thereof. He shall at least twice during the week go through the prison at an uncertain hour of the night, which visit, with the hour and state of the prison at the time, he shall record in his journal. When visiting the females' prison he shall be attended by the matron or some other female officer. — *To inspect the prison daily.*

67. The Governor shall cause an abstract, to be approved by the Lord Lieutenant, of the regulations relating to the treatment and conduct of prisoners, with a copy of the prison dietaries (printed in legible characters) to be posted in each cell, and shall read or cause the same to be read to every prisoner who cannot read within 24 hours after his admission, and subsequently once in each month. — *To post up in cells abstract of certain regulations.*

68. The Governor shall without delay call the attention of the surgeon to any prisoner whose state of mind or body appears to require attention, and shall carry into effect the written directions of the surgeon respecting alterations of the discipline or treatment of any such prisoner. — *To report to surgeon prisoners disordered in mind.*

69. The

To notify to Chaplain and Surgeon prisoners requiring their attention.

69. The Governor shall notify to the surgeon without delay the illness of any prisoner, and shall deliver to him daily a list of such prisoners as complain of illness, or are removed to the infirmary or confined to their cell by illness, and he shall daily deliver to the Chaplain and Surgeon lists of such prisoners as are confined to punishment cells.

To give notice of death of prisoners.

70. The Governor, upon the death of a prisoner, shall give immediate notice thereof to the coroner of the district to which the prison belongs, to the General Prisons Board, and to one of the Visiting Committee, as well as to the nearest relative of the deceased, where procurable.

To report to Visiting Committee insane prisoners.

71. The Governor shall without delay report to the Visiting Committee any case of insanity or apparent insanity occurring among the prisoners.

To keep accustomed books and accounts.

72. The Governor shall keep all such records, accounts, reports, and returns as are required by the rules, or as may be directed from time to time by the General Prisons Board.

To be responsible for safe custody of documents. Not to be absent without leave.

73. The Governor shall be responsible for the proper keeping and safe custody of the journals, registers, books, commitments, and all other documents confided to his care.

74. The Governor shall not be absent from the prison for a night without permission in writing from the General Prisons Board, and his leave of absence shall be entered in his journal; but if absent without leave for a night from unavoidable necessity he shall state the fact and the cause of it in his journal, reporting immediately to the General Prisons Board.

Power of Deputy Governor.

75. Where a Deputy Governor is appointed to a prison he shall be legally competent to perform any duty required by law to be performed by the Governor, and when the Governor is absent from the prison the Deputy Governor shall perform all his duties. Where there is no Deputy Governor, or in case of his services not being available by reason of sickness or other unavoidable cause, the Governor shall, when absent from the prison on leave, appoint, with the consent of the General Prisons Board, as officer of the prison to act as his substitute, and during such absence the substitute so appointed shall have all the powers and perform all the duties of the Governor.

Substitute of Deputy Governor.

The Deputy Governor when in charge of the prison as Governor shall, if absent from the prison from any unavoidable cause, or unable from sickness to perform his duties, appoint a substitute with the sanction of the General Prisons Board.

To appoint himself with Acts of Parliament and prison rules.

76. The Governor shall supply the copies of all Acts of Parliament in force which relate to any part of his duties, or to the management of prisons, or the treatment of prisoners, and for a copy of the rules in force in the prison.

Conduct to prisoners.

77. The Governor shall exercise his authority with firmness and humanity, and shall enforce similar conduct on the other officers.

Complaints from prisoners.

78. The Governor shall at all times be ready to receive any complaint or application of a prisoner.

To read certain rules to prisoners.

79. The Governor shall read or cause to be read to each male prisoner on admission, and to all the male prisoners once a month, such rules as may be prescribed by the General Prisons Board.

To direct the distribution of food.

80. The Governor shall direct the distribution of food according to the prescribed scales of diet, and shall cause any article of food to be weighed or measured, if so required by a prisoner.

Inspection of provisions.

81. The Governor or his deputy shall examine all articles of provisions brought into the prison for the use of the prisoners, before received over by the storekeeper.

Governor's Order Book.

82. The Governor shall enter in a book, to be called "The Governor's Order Book," all his orders relating to the discipline of the prison.

To pay over fines.

83. The Governor shall in the case of the payment of any fine or penalty, subject to any existing lien or right, as early as practicable, pay over the same to the person authorised to receive it.

Jew prisoners.

84. The Governor shall see that no Jew be required to labour on his Sabbath.

Insane prisoners.

85. The Governor shall take such necessary steps as may be within his power to have all insane prisoners removed from the prison as speedily as the law will allow.

To keep witnesses on behalf of the Crown separate from others.

86. The Governor shall see that persons in his custody intended to be examined as witnesses on behalf of the Crown are kept separate from any other class of prisoners.

To lay the journal before the Visiting Committee.

87. The Governor shall invariably lay his journal before the Visiting Committee at their visits.

To be present at unlocking and at unlocking.

88. The Governor shall be present at the unlocking of his prison, and he or the chief warder shall be present at locking.

Shall see to carry out time table.

89. The Governor shall take care that the time table authorised by the General Prisons Board shall be strictly adhered to.

90. The

92. The Governor shall take every precaution necessary for preventing escape, and shall cause a daily examination to be made of the cell windows, bars, bolts, locks, &c.; and he shall require each day at lock-up, certificates from all warders in charge of wards that such examinations has been carefully made by them. He shall see that no ladders, planks, wheelbarrows, ropes, chains, implements, or materials of any kind likely to facilitate escape are left unnecessarily exposed at any time in the yards or elsewhere. All such articles, when not in use, must be kept in their appointed places. He shall also adopt proper precautions against fire, and take care that the appliances for its prevention are kept in an effective state, and that the proper officers and the prisoners are periodically exercised in working them. He shall take care that a proper supply of water is at all times maintained

[margin: Security of the prisoners, and precautions against fire.]

THE CHAPLAIN.

91. [Revoked. See amended Rules for Chaplains, page 21.]

92. The Chaplain shall more particularly afford his spiritual assistance to all prisoners under order for execution, or committed on charges punishable with death.
[margin: To attend prisoners ordered for execution.]

93. The Chaplain shall see and admonish every prisoner under charge or conviction of any crime, on admission and discharge, so far as practicable.
[margin: To see prisoners on admission and discharge.]

94. The Chaplain shall pay particular attention to the state of mind of every prisoner; and if he observe that the mind of any prisoner is likely to be injuriously affected by the discipline or treatment, he shall report the same in writing to the Governor, entering such report in his journal.
[margin: To pay particular attention to every prisoner's state of mind.]

95. The Chaplain shall frequently visit the schools and inspect the course of instruction pursued in them; but any examination of the prisoners at school which he may make shall be confined to the subjects of the books of lessons, and shall be of a secular character. If he shall find any cause for complaint, he shall make it known to the Governor, or if necessary, to the General Prison Board. He shall see that the School Register is properly kept, and note the progress of the prisoners separately therein. He shall not introduce for prison use any book or other publication or document which has not been sanctioned by the General Prison Board.
[margin: To visit school and examine the prisoners.]

96. The Chaplain shall keep an accurate register of the burials of all prisoners belonging to his persuasion who may die in the prison, and he shall, if required, attend at the interment of each prisoner.
[margin: Burials.]

97. The Chaplain shall keep a journal noting his attendance, and the several duties performed by him, and invariably lay it before the Visiting Committee at their visits.
[margin: Journal.]

98. The Chaplain shall communicate to the Governor any abuse or impropriety in the prison which may come to his knowledge, and shall enter the same in his journal.
[margin: Chaplain to communicate abuses to Governor.]

99. [Revoked. See amended Rules for Chaplains, page 21.]

100. In the event of the death of any Chaplain or Assistant Chaplain of a prison, the Governor shall provide a substitute, and report the vacancy to the General Prison Board.
[margin: Substitute on death of chaplain or absence.]

THE SURGEON.*

THE MATRON.

101. The Matron shall be under the direction of the Governor, and shall reside in the prison. She shall have the care and superintendence of the whole female department. The wards, cells, and yards where females are confined shall be secured by locks different from those securing the wards, cells, and yards allotted to male prisoners, and the keys of these locks shall be kept in the custody of the Matron.
[margin: General duties.]

102. The Matron shall visit and inspect every part of the prison occupied by females, and see every female prisoner once at least in every 24 hours, and in default of such daily visits and inspections she shall state in her journal how far she has omitted them, and the cause thereof. She shall at least twice during the week, go through each part of the prison at an uncertain hour of the night, which visit, with the hour, and state of each part of the prison at the time, shall be recorded in her journal.
[margin: To inspect daily female prisoners.]

103. The Matron shall not be absent from the prison for a night without permission in writing from the General Prison Board on the recommendation of the Governor; and her
[margin: Not to be absent without leave.]

---

* See Rules for Surgeons, pages 23-28.

her leave of absence shall be entered in her journal; but if absent without leave for a night from unavoidable necessity, she shall state the fact and the cause of it in her journal, the Governor reporting the same to the General Prisons Board.

To appoint deputy when absent. 104. The Matron shall, with the consent of the Governor, and with the approval of the General Prisons Board, appoint a female officer of the prison to act as Deputy Matron whenever she is absent on leave from the prison, and during such absence the Deputy Matron shall have all the powers and duties of the Matron. Before leaving the prison the Matron shall personally give over the charge of the part of the prison occupied by females to the Deputy Matron.

To keep journal. 105. The Matron shall keep a journal in which she shall record all occurrences of importance within her department, and punishments of female prisoners, and lay the journal before the Governor daily, and before the Visiting Committee at their visits.

Issue of provisions. 106. The Matron shall exercise a careful supervision over the issue of provisions to the prisoners according to their respective class diets.

To attend Divine Service. 107. The Matron shall attend Divine Service with the prisoners unless absent by leave or prevented by some duty; inserting the explanation and cause thereof in her journal.

To attend male officers and visitors on their visits to the female prison. 108. The Matron shall, unless unavoidably prevented, attend the Governor whenever he visits the female prison, and when so prevented, she shall be responsible that some other female officer attends him; and she shall take care that no male officer or visitor enters the females' prison, unless accompanied by herself or by some other female officer.

To read rules to prisoners. 109. The Matron shall read, or cause to be read, to each female prisoner, on admission and to all the female prisoners once a month, such rules as may be prescribed by the General Prisons Board.

To search female visitors to prisoners. 110. The Matron, or in her absence some other female officer, shall, whenever she thinks it necessary, or when directed by the Governor, search any female visitor to prisoners; the search to be in the presence of females only and not in the presence of any prisoner.

Daily report. 111. The Matron shall make a daily written report to the Governor, at some stated time fixed by him, of the general condition and conduct of her department; of the names of female officers and prisoners absent from chapel, and the cause thereof.

PRISON OFFICERS.

Regulation as to employment of prisoners in prison office. 112. No prisoner shall be employed as Turnkey, Assistant Turnkey, Overseer, Monitor, or Schoolmaster, or in the discipline of the prison, or in the service of any officer thereof, or in the service or instruction of any other prisoner. But this regulation shall not be taken to prevent the employment of any debtor in that part of the prison in which he may be lawfully confined, in any manner in which he may be willing to be employed, and which is consistent with his safe custody.

Prison officers to be constables. 113. Every prison officer, while acting as such, shall, by virtue of his appointment, and without being sworn in before any justice, be deemed to be a constable, and to have all such powers, authorities, protection, and privileges for the purpose of the execution of his duty as a prison officer as any constable duly appointed has within his constable-wick by Common Law, Statute, or Custom.

Officers not to sell or let to prisoners. 114. No officer of a prison shall sell or let to, nor shall any person in trust for or employed by him sell or let to, or derive any benefit from the selling or letting of any article to any prisoner.

Officers not to contract with prisoners. 115. No officer of a prison shall, nor shall any person in trust for or employed by him have any interest, direct or indirect, in any contract for the supply of the prison.

Officers not to take gratuities. 116. No officer of a prison shall at any time receive money, fee, or gratuity of any kind for the admission of any visitor to the prison or to prisoners, or from or on behalf of any prisoner, on any pretext whatever.

117. In every prison female prisoners shall be attended by female officers.

Officers to obey Governor. 118. All officers of the prison shall obey the directions of the Governor, so far as they consist with prison rules, and all subordinate officers shall perform such duties as may be directed by the Governor, with the sanction of the General Prisons Board, and the duties of each subordinate officer shall be inserted in a book to be kept by him.

Not to be absent without leave. 119. Subordinate officers shall not be absent from the prison without leave from the Governor, and before absenting themselves they shall leave their keys, instruction book, and report book in the Governor's office.

Not to receive visitors without leave. 120. Subordinate officers shall not be permitted to receive any visitors within the prison without permission of the Governor.

121. Subordinate

181. Subordinate officers shall frequently examine the state of the cells, bedding, locks, bolts, &c., and shall seize all prohibited articles, and deliver them to the Governor forthwith. *To examine cells, locks, &c.*

182. It is the duty of all officers to treat the prisoners with kindness and humanity, to listen patiently to and report their complaints or grievances, being firm at the same time in maintaining order and discipline, and enforcing complete observance of the rules and regulations of the prison. *Treatment of prisoners.*

183. Officers shall duly inform the Governor of any prisoner who desires to see him, or to make any complaint or prefer any request to him or to any superior authority. Any neglect in carrying out this instruction will be most severely dealt with. *Prisoners desiring to make complaint.*

184. It shall be the duty of every officer to direct the attention of the Governor to any prisoner who may appear to him sick or in health, although he may not complain; or whose state of mind may appear to him deserving of special notice and care, in order that the opinion and instructions of the medical officer may be taken on the case. *Report as to sick or lunatic prisoners.*

185. No officer shall strike a prisoner, unless compelled to do so in self-defence. *Prisoners not to be struck.*

186. No subordinate officer, on any pretence whatever, through favour, or mistaken notions of kindness, shall fail to make an immediate report to the Governor, or other his superior officer, of any misconduct or wilful disobedience of the prison regulations. *Misconduct to be reported without delay.*

187. No subordinate officer shall unnecessarily converse with a prisoner, nor allow any familiarity on the part of prisoners towards himself or any other officer or servant of the prison; nor shall he on any account speak of his duties, or of any matters of discipline or prison arrangement, within the hearing of the prisoners. *Officers not to converse with prisoners.*

188. No officer shall have any pecuniary dealing whatsoever with any prisoner, or employ any prisoner on his private account, nor shall he correspond with or hold any intercourse with the friends or relatives of any prisoner, unless expressly authorised by the Governor; nor shall he make any unauthorised communications concerning the prison to any person whatever. *Officers not to have pecuniary dealings with prisoners.*

189. All officers shall be careful not to allow any prisoners under their charge to be employed, directly or indirectly, for the private benefit or advantage of any person or persons, or in any way not in conformity to the rules of the prison. *Prisoners not to be employed for private benefit.*

190. All officers will be held responsible for being fully acquainted with the rules and orders relating to their respective duties. They shall strictly conform to and obey the orders of the Governor in every respect. They shall assist him in maintaining order and discipline among the prisoners. For this end, punishment for prison offences must sometimes be resorted to by the Governor upon their report; but good temper and good example, on the part of the officers and servants, will have great influence in preventing the frequent recurrence of offences, and the necessity for such punishments. *Officers to make themselves acquainted with prison rules.*

191. Every prison officer shall treat the members of the Visiting Committee with the greatest courtesy and respect. Any infringement of this rule will render the offender liable to severe punishment. *Conduct to visiting committee.*

192. Every officer who shall be in charge of any prisoner to be brought for trial before a court, shall carefully search the person of such prisoner, in order to prevent the concealment of any weapon of offence, or missile, and shall maintain a watchful supervision over such prisoner during his trial. *Search of prisoner leaving gaol for trial.*

193. Any officer desiring to appeal against any decision which affects him, or wishing to bring any matter before superior authority, will state his complaint in such manner as may be provided by the regulations for the consideration of the General Prisons Board. Such complaint to be made within one week of such decision. *Complaints to be made within one week.*

194. No officer shall use tobacco or spirituous liquors within the prison walls, except under such restrictions as to time and place as may be laid down by the Governor and approved by the General Prisons Board. *Tobacco or spirituous liquors not to be used by officers within prison.*

195. Every officer who shall bring in or carry out, or endeavour to bring in or carry out, or knowingly allow to be brought in or carried out to or for any prisoner, any money, clothing, provisions, tobacco, letters, papers, or other articles whatsoever, shall be forthwith suspended from his office by the Governor of the Prison, who shall report the offence to the General Prisons Board. *Officers not to bring in prohibited articles.*

196. Fines may be levied by the General Prisons Board and the Governor upon all subordinate officers and servants of the establishment for misconduct, neglect of rules or duty, according to a scale to be prescribed by General Prisons Board, and approved by the Lord Lieutenant. *Fines on officers by Governor.*

197. Servants or officers whose services are discontinued (except such as are temporarily engaged, or who have not completed their probation, or are at weekly wages, or shall be dismissed for misconduct), shall be entitled to one month's notice or a month's pay. In like manner, officers shall be required to give one month's notice before leaving. *Payment of discontinued officers.*

Duties of gate porter.

138. The officer acting as gate porter may examine all articles carried in or out of the prison, and shall stop any person suspected of bringing in spirits or other prohibited articles into the prison, or of carrying out any property belonging to the prison, giving immediate notice thereof to the Governor.

Names of persons desirous to see the Governor.

139. Subordinate officers shall without delay, give to the Governor in writing the name of any prisoner who may desire to see the Governor, the Chaplain, or a member of the Visiting Committee.

To carry out strictly the orders given.

140. Subordinate officers shall by every means in their power prevent prisoners from holding any communication with each other at any time, either by speaking, by signs, or by stratagem, and shall report to the Governor any disobedience of this rule.

Conduct to prisoners.

141. Subordinate officers shall exercise their authority with firmness, temper and humanity, and abstain from irritating language, at the same time avoiding the least approach to familiarity of conversation, on any subject whatever.

Reports in writing to the Governor.

142. Each male officer in charge of a department or ward of the prison, shall daily report to the Governor, in writing, the condition of his department or ward, and the female officer shall in like manner report to the Matron. In all cases of emergency the officer shall report verbally, without delay, and subsequently make an entry thereof in the report book.

Resident officer.

143. No subordinate resident officer (either male or female) shall be absent from the prison for the night without the previous permission of the Governor, unless from unavoidable circumstances to be explained.

Not allow a visitor without an order.

144. No officer, without a special order of the Governor, shall allow any visitor to see a prisoner in his cell, nor allow a visitor to speak to, or have any communication with, a prisoner.

Meals.

145. The subordinate officers shall take their meals at such times and under such regulations as the General Prisons Board may direct.

Definition of subordinate officers.

146. All officers of a prison shall be deemed to be subordinate officers with the exception of the Gaoler, the Chaplains, the Surgeon, and the Matron.

147. All prison officers shall on appointment make themselves acquainted with the prison rules.

MISCELLANEOUS.

Miscellaneous.

148. No visitor shall enter the prison or look through the buildings without the written permission of the Visiting Committee, or of the General Prisons Board to do so.

Record of visits of chaplain and non-resident officers.

149. There shall be kept in every prison a book, to be called the non-resident officers' book, in which the Chaplain and any other officer of the prison not residing within the prison, but attending or required to attend such prison, shall regularly enter the date of every visit made to the prison by such officer; and every entry shall be signed with the name and in the handwriting of such officer.

150. The foregoing rules shall apply to every ordinary prison, and shall come into operation upon the expiration of 40 days after the same, having been settled and approved by the Lord Lieutenant and Privy Council, shall have been laid before Parliament.

(End.)

Made and executed this 22nd day of March 1878, by " The General Prisons Board for Ireland."

Walter Crofton, Chairman.

By the Lord Lieutenant and Privy Council of Ireland.

Marlborough.

In pursuance of the General Prisons (Ireland) Act, 1877, We, John Winston, Duke of Marlborough, Lord Lieutenant General and General Governor of Ireland, with the approval, advice, and consent of the Privy Council of Ireland, have settled, and hereby approve of, the foregoing general rules for the government of prisons, made by the General Prisons Board for Ireland.

Dated this 22nd day of March 1878.

Given at the Council Chamber in Dublin Castle.

J. T. Ball, C.
Walter Crofton.
J. Michel, General.
Edward Gibson.

By the Lord Lieutenant General and General Governor of Ireland.

Marlborough.

In pursuance of the General Prisons (Ireland) Act, 1877, We, John Winston, Duke of Marlborough, Lord Lieutenant-General and General Governor of Ireland, do hereby make and publish the following Rule with respect to visiting committees of prisons, that is to say :—

Where a visiting committee consists of nine or more members, a quorum of such committee shall consist of three members ; and where a visiting committee consists of less than nine members, a quorum of such committee shall consist of two members ; and no act of any meeting of a visiting committee shall be valid, unless a quorum of its members shall be present thereat.

(Given at Her Majesty's Castle at Dublin, this 2nd day of January 1878.

By his Grace's Command,

T. H. Burke.

THE CHAPLAIN.

By the General Prisons Board for Ireland.

In pursuance of the General Prisons (Ireland) Act, 1877, the General Prisons Board for Ireland hereby makes the following amended General Rules for the Government of Prisons :—

The Chaplain.

1. The Chaplain shall see the sick and visit the prisoners, if any, confined in punishment cells, at least three times a week, Sundays included, and oftener if necessary, and shall pay special attention to juvenile offenders.

To visit the sick and prisoners in punishment cells at least three times a week.

2. The General Prisons Board may, upon the application of any chaplain, approve of certain clergymen, not exceeding three in number, of the same religious persuasion as such chaplain, from whom he may appoint a substitute or substitutes, or accept assistance under the circumstances, and in the cases hereinafter provided.

Chaplain's substitute to be approved by Prisons Board.

3. The chaplain shall insert the names and residences of the clergymen so approved of in the chaplain's journal.

Names of substitutes to be entered in Journal.

4. The chaplain, when he is absent on leave, or when, from sickness or other sufficient cause, he is prevented from performing his duties in person, may nominate one or more of the clergymen so approved of as his substitute or substitutes, or may accept the assistance of any of the said clergymen in performance of his duties.

Substitution by chaplain of substitutes.

5. The General Prisons Board may withdraw an approval given under Rule No. 2.

6. The 91st and 99th of the Rules for Local Prisons in Ireland, approved by Order in Council, dated the 23rd day of March 1878, are hereby revoked, and these Rules are substituted therefor.

The foregoing Rules shall apply to every ordinary Prison, and shall come into operation upon the expiration of forty days after the same, having been settled and approved by the Lord Lieutenant and Privy Council, shall have been laid before Parliament.

Made and executed this 5th day of May 1879, by " The General Prisons Board for Ireland."

Charles F. Bourke, Chairman.

By the Lords Justices and Privy Council of Ireland.

J. T. Ball, C.
Hedges Eyre Chatterton.

In pursuance of the General Prisons (Ireland) Act, 1877, We, the Lords Justices General and General Governors of Ireland, with the approval, advice, and consent of the Privy Council of Ireland, have settled and hereby approve of the foregoing rules made by the General Prisons Board for Ireland.
Dated this 24th day of June 1879.

Given at the Council Chamber in Dublin Castle.

M. Morris.
Henry Ormsby.

By the General Prisons Board for Ireland.

In pursuance of the General Prisons (Ireland) Act, 1877, the General Prisons Board hereby make the following Amended Rules for the Government of Prisons:—

I. Addendum to Rule 24 (General Rules for the Government of Prisons):—

For the purpose of this rule, a prisoner in custody under sentence for consecutive terms of imprisonment which in the aggregate exceed one month, shall be considered as a prisoner whose sentence exceeds one month.

II. Addendum to Rule 28:

The word "sentence" in this rule includes the period, or the aggregate of the periods, during which a male prisoner above 16 years of age sentenced to hard labour is to be retained in custody, whether under one, or more than one committal.

III. Districts for Local Prisons:

The word "term" in schedule to "Rules for the Districts of Local Prisons in Ireland" shall include the period, or aggregate of the periods, during which a convicted prisoner is to be retained in custody, whether under one, or more than one, committal.

The foregoing rules shall apply to the prisoners confined in every ordinary prison, and shall come into operation upon the expiration of forty days after the same, having been settled and approved by the Lord Lieutenant, or Lords Justices and Privy Council, shall have been laid before Parliament.

Made and approved this 6th day of April 1883, by "The General Prisons Board for Ireland."

J. Barton, Vice-Chairman. [Seal.]

By the Lord Lieutenant and Privy Council of Ireland.

Cowper.

In pursuance of the General Prisons (Ireland) Act, 1877, We, Francis Thomas De Grey, Earl Cowper, Lord Lieutenant-General and General Governor of Ireland, with the approval, advice, and consent of the Privy Council of Ireland, have settled and hereby approve of the foregoing rules made by the General Prisons Board for Ireland.

Given at the Council Chamber, Dublin Castle, this 30th day of April 1883.

H. Law, C.
Lobster.
Belmore.
Henry Ormsby.

THE SURGEON.

By the General Prisons Board for Ireland.

In pursuance of the General Prisons (Ireland) Act, 1877, the General Prisons Board for Ireland hereby makes the following amended General Rules for the Government of Prisons:—

1. [Annulled. See amended Rule for Surgeons, No. 2, page 62.]

2. The surgeon shall enter, in the English language, day by day, in his journal to be kept in the prison, on account of the state of every sick prisoner, the name of his disease, a description of the medicines and diet, and any other treatment which he may order for each prisoner.

3. The surgeon shall, once at least in every three months, inspect every part of the prison, and enter in his journal the result of such inspection, recording therein any observations he may think fit to make on any want of cleanliness, drainage, warmth, or ventilation; any bad quality of the provisions, any insufficiency of clothing or bedding, any deficiency in the quantity or defect in the quality of the water, or any other cause which may affect the health of the prisoners.

4. Whenever

4. Whenever the surgeon has reason to believe that the mind of a prisoner is, or is likely to be injuriously affected by the discipline or treatment, he shall report the case in writing to the governor, together with such directions as he may think proper, and he shall call the attention of the chaplain to any prisoner who appears to require his special notice.
To report special cases.

5. The surgeon may in any case of danger or difficulty which appears to him to require it, call in additional medical assistance; and no serious operation shall be performed without a previous consultation being held with another medical practitioner, except under circumstances not admitting of delay, such circumstances to be recorded in his journal, and reported to the General Prisons Board.
To call in additional medical aid.

6. The surgeon shall, forthwith, on the death of any prisoner, enter in his journal the following particulars, viz.: at what time the deceased was taken ill, when the illness was first communicated to the surgeon, the nature of the disease, when the prisoner died, and an account of the appearances after death (in cases where a post-mortem examination is made), together with any special remarks that appear to him to be required.
To make entries as to death of prisoner.

7. In case of sickness, or unavoidable absence, or leave, to be given by the General Prisons Board, the surgeon shall appoint a fully qualified substitute, approved of by the General Prisons Board. The name and residence of the substitute shall be entered in his journal.
To appoint substitute when absent.

8. The surgeon shall examine every prisoner before he is passed into the proper ward; and shall record the prisoner's name, age, state of health on admission, and any disease of importance to which he may have been subject.
To examine every prisoner on admission.

9. The surgeon may direct the supply of flannels and such other things as he may deem requisite, in cases where the health of the prisoner, in his opinion, is suffering by the want of them.
Supply of flannels.

10. The surgeon shall examine every prisoner sentenced to hard labour, and shall certify whether any such prisoner is unfit to be kept at it, and he shall from time to time examine the prisoners during the time of their being employed at hard labour, and shall enter in his journal the name of any prisoner whose health he thinks to be endangered by a continuance at it, and thereupon such prisoner shall not again be employed at hard labour until the surgeon certifies that he is fit for such employment.
Examination of prisoners at hard labour.

11. The surgeon shall inspect each prisoner before put to tread-wheel labour, and report, for the governor's information and guidance, his fitness or otherwise for such labour.
To inspect prisoner previous to being put to labour on the tread-wheel.

12. The surgeon shall direct that every prisoner take daily as much exercise in the open air as may be necessary for health.
Exercise in the open air.

13. The surgeon shall give directions in writing for separating prisoners having infectious complaints, or being suspected thereof; for cleansing, disinfecting, and whitewashing any apartments occupied by such prisoners, and for washing, disinfecting, or destroying any infected apparel or bedding.
To give directions in case of infection.

14. [Annulled. See amended Rule for Surgeons, No. 2, page 21.]

15. The surgeon shall, when required by the General Prisons Board, furnish a report as to the physical fitness of any candidate for employment in the prison's service, and shall also, from time to time, furnish to the Civil Service Commissioners such detailed information in reference to the health, &c., of a candidate as such Commissioners consider necessary, in order to enable them to issue their certificate of qualification.
To make reports as to fitness physically of candidates.

The foregoing rules shall apply to every ordinary prison, and shall come into operation upon the expiration of 40 days after the same, having been settled and approved by the Lord Lieutenant and Privy Council, shall have been laid before Parliament.

Made and executed this 14th day of November 1877, by "The General Prisons Board for Ireland."

Charles F. Bourke, Chairman.   [Seal]

By the Lord Lieutenant and Privy Council of Ireland.

Spencer.

In pursuance of the General Prisons (Ireland) Act, 1877, We, John Poyntz, Earl Spencer, Lord Lieutenant General and General Governor of Ireland, with the approval, advice, and consent of the Privy Council of Ireland, have settled, and hereby approve of the foregoing Rules made by the General Prisons Board for Ireland.

Given at the Council Chamber in Dublin Castle, this 13th day of November 1883.

> H. Law, C.
> *Leinster.*
> *Monck.*
> W. H. F. Cogan.
> S. Wenslyn Flanagan.
> Henry Ormsby.
> O'Conor Don.
> Thos. Shaek, Genl.

SPECIAL RULE FOR PRISONERS AWAITING TRIAL.

By the General Prisons Board for Ireland.

In pursuance of the General Prisons (Ireland) Act, 1877, the General Prisons Board for Ireland hereby order that the Special Rule made the 7th day of May 1883, amending the 18th of the Special Rules for Prisoners awaiting trial, made the 22nd day of March 1876,* shall be revoked, and in lieu thereof that it be ordered that the 18th of the Special Rules for Prisoners awaiting trial, made the 22nd day of March 1876, shall be amended, by adding thereto as follows:—

Provided always that the Lord Lieutenant, or other Chief Governor or Governors of Ireland for the time being, may suspend and withdraw the permission hereby granted in any case when he or they consider it necessary so to do for the purpose of the security, good order, and government of the prison and prisoners therein, or for the purpose of preventing any tampering with evidence, or any plans for escape, or other like considerations.

Made and executed this 7th day of November 1884 by the General Prisons Board for Ireland.

     [*Seal.*]

> Charles F. Bourke,
> Chairman.

By the Lord Lieutenant and Privy Council in Ireland.

Spencer.

In pursuance of the General Prisons (Ireland) Act, 1877, We, John Poyntz, Earl Spencer, Lord Lieutenant General and General Governor of Ireland, with the approval, advice, and consent of the Privy Council of Ireland, have settled, and hereby approve of the foregoing Special Rule, with respect to prisoners awaiting trial, made by the General Prisons Board for Ireland.

Given at the Council Chamber, Dublin Castle, the 15th day of November 1884.

> Edward Sullivan, C.
> W. H. F. Cogan.
> A. M. Porter.
> *Leinster.*
> Thos. Shaek, Gen.
> John Naish.

By the General Prisons Board for Ireland.

In pursuance of the General Prisons (Ireland) Act, 1877, the General Prisons Board for Ireland do hereby direct that the Special Rules with respect to prisoners awaiting trial, bearing date the 22nd day of March 1876, shall be altered and added to as follows:—

1. The Governor shall, on the application of any such prisoner, allow him the use, from time to time, of library books provided for the use of prisoners.

            II. The

---

* See Rule 18, p. 8.

II. The Governor shall, subject to the approval of the Visiting Committee, permit any such prisoner to smoke while at exercise in the open air, provided he is satisfied that he has been in the habit of smoking previous to committal.

III. The Governor shall permit the light to remain burning in the cell of any such prisoner to enable the prisoner to continue to read or write, or to work and follow his trade, until the final lacking-up of the prison provided any reasonable or satisfactory ground exists for the allowance of such privilege. The Governor to report to the Board and to the Visiting Committee for their approval all cases in which he grants this privilege.

IV. Such prisoners if detained in custody awaiting trial for more than three months are to be granted such relaxations as to dietary and hours of exercise in the open air as may be considered requisite by the Medical Officer, subject to the approval of the Board.

V. The granting of the several privileges aforesaid is to be subject to the provisions contained in the 6th of the said Special Rules of the 22nd day of March 1878.*

Made and examined this 13th day of March 1885, by the General Prisons Board for Ireland.

Charles F. Bowie, Chairman.

By the Lord Lieutenant and Privy Council of Ireland.

Spencer.

In pursuance of the General Prisons (Ireland) Act, 1877, We, John Poyntz Earl Spencer, Lord Lieutenant General and General Governor of Ireland, with the approval, advice, and consent of the Privy Council of Ireland, have ratified and hereby approve of the foregoing Special Rules made by the General Prisons Board for Ireland with respect to prisoners awaiting trial.

Given at the Council Chamber, Dublin Castle, this 15th day of March 1885.

Edward Sullivan, C.
John Naish.

GENERAL RULES FOR PRISONERS

By the General Prisons Board for Ireland.

In pursuance of the General Prisons (Ireland) Act, 1877, the General Prisons Board for Ireland do hereby direct that the General Rules for the government of Prisons, dated the 22nd day of March 1877, and the General Rules in relation to the duties of Surgeons to Prisons, dated the 18th day of November 1882, shall be altered and added to as follows, that is to say:—The 61st of the said first-mentioned Rules, and the 1st and 14th of the said secondly-mentioned Rules, are hereby annulled, and in lieu thereof it is hereby ordered:

1. That no irons or means of mechanical restraint shall be used excepting such as are approved by the Lord Lieutenant, or such as may be considered necessary by the Medical Officer to be used as medical appliances in the case of violent prisoners in hospitals.

2. The Surgeon shall visit the prison once each day, and not later than 10 o'clock, noon, and oftener if necessary, and shall see every prisoner in the course of the week. He shall daily visit the prisoners, if any, confined in punishment cells, or under punishments in their own cells, or under mechanical restraint, and he shall visit daily, and oftener if necessary, such of the prisoners as are sick, and, when necessary, shall direct any prisoner to be removed to the infirmary.

3. The Surgeon shall, whenever he considers a prisoner's life to be in danger by further confinement, at once report the fact to the Under Secretary, for the Lord Lieutenant's information, and also to the General Prisons Board, and to the Governor, and he is also to report to the Governor the case of any prisoner to which he may think it necessary, on medical grounds, to draw attention.

Made and examined this 13th day of March 1885, by "The General Prisons Board for Ireland."

Charles F. Bowie, Chairman.

* See p. 4.

By the Lord Lieutenant and Privy Council of Ireland.

Spencer.

In pursuance of the General Prisons (Ireland) Act, 1877, We, John Poyntz, Earl Spencer, Lord Lieutenant General and General Governor of Ireland, with the approval, advice, and consent of the Privy Council of Ireland, have settled and hereby approve of the foregoing Rules made by the General Prisons Board for Ireland.

Given at the Council Chamber, Dublin Castle, this 13th day of March 1884.

Edward Sullivan, C.
John Naish.

RULE AS TO PUNISHMENT AND CLASSIFICATION OF PRISONERS.

By the General Prisons Board for Ireland.

In pursuance of the General Prisons (Ireland) Act, 1877, the General Prisons Board for Ireland hereby make the following Amended Rule for the Government of Prisons:—

Addenda to Rule 59 of General Rules for prisoners in local prisons, Ireland:—

Any criminal prisoner punished by the visiting committee, or by a justice having jurisdiction in the place to which the prison belongs, shall, in addition to any other punishment, be liable to a reduction in classification or loss of marks, if the Prisons Board see fit so to order. It shall be competent to the Prisons Board to restore to the said prisoner, as a reward for subsequent good conduct, the classification or marks of which he may be so deprived.

The foregoing Rule shall apply to the prisoners confined in every ordinary prison, and shall come into operation upon the expiration of 40 days after the same, having been settled and approved by the Lord Lieutenant or Lords Justices and Privy Council, shall have been laid before Parliament.

Made and examined this 26th day of March 1884, by the " General Prisons Board for Ireland."

Charles F. Bourke, Chairman.

[Seal]

By the Lord Lieutenant and Privy Council, Ireland.

Aberdeen.

In pursuance of the General Prisons (Ireland) Act, 1877, We, John Campbell, Earl of Aberdeen, Lord Lieutenant General and General Governor of Ireland, with the approval, advice, and consent of the Privy Council of Ireland, have settled, and hereby approve of the foregoing Rule with respect to the punishment and classification of prisoners made by the General Prisons Board for Ireland.

Given at the Council Chamber, Dublin Castle, the 11th day of May 1884.

Edwd. Sugg-Winser, General.
John Naish, C.
S. Woulfe Flanagan.
P. J. Keenan.
R. Dunne.
Samuel Walker.
J. Lentaigne.

RELIGIOUS INSTRUCTION.

By the General Prisons Board for Ireland.

In pursuance of the General Prisons (Ireland) Act, 1877, the General Prisons Board for Ireland do hereby direct that the General Rules for the Government of Prisons, dated the 22nd day of March 1878, shall be altered, as follows, that is to say:—The 49th of the said Rules is hereby annulled, and in lieu thereof it is hereby ordered:

49. The Governor may, by writing under his hand, provisionally permit a prisoner to be attended by a minister of any religious denomination, other than the religious denominations which respectively have a gaol chaplain or chaplains attached to the gaol, under such regulations as may from time to time be established. The Governor, whenever he grants such permission, shall at once forward a full report of the circumstances of the case to the General Prisons Board, who may withdraw or suspend such permission as they may think fit.

Made and executed this 17th day of April 1889, by "The General Prisons Board for Ireland."

Charles F. Bourke, Chairman.

[Seal.]

By the Lords Justices and Privy Council in Ireland.

Edward Sam-Weiner, General.
Hedges Eyre Chatterton.
John T. Ball.

In pursuance of the General Prisons (Ireland) Act, 1877, We, the Lords Justices General and General Governors of Ireland, with the approval, advice, and consent of the Privy Council of Ireland, have settled and hereby approve of the foregoing Rule made by the General Prisons Board for Ireland.

Given at the Council Chamber, Dublin Castle, this 30th day of April 1889.

Ashbourne, C.
Ashtown.
Peter O'Brien.

LOCAL PRISONS OF IRELAND.

SCALE of FINES on SUBORDINATE OFFICERS.

FINES may be levied by the Governor upon all the subordinate officers and servants of the establishment as for neglect of duty. Such fines to be disposed of as may from time to time be directed by the General Prisons Board.

1. Coming late to duty, any time not exceeding five minutes; each offence, 3 d., and 6 d. for each additional five minutes.

2. Leaving a cell or principal door unlocked.

3. Entering a prisoner's cell at night contrary to orders.

4. Allowing any unauthorised person to communicate with a prisoner within or outside the prison walls.

5. Leaving prisoners in the halls, wards, prison grounds, exercising yards, or other where within or outside the prison walls, unattended by an officer or other authorised person.

6. Cursing, swearing, or using indecent or immoral language.

7. Allowing tools lying about in the part of the prison under their charge or superintendence, ladders or anything likely to facilitate the escape of a prisoner.

8. Sleeping whilst on duty, by day.
    1st offence, 3 s.; 2nd offence, 6 s.; 3rd offence, suspension.

9. Leaving a cell, or passage, or other door singly locked, which ought to be double-locked.

10. Leaving a passage or other door (not included in No. 9) unlocked.

11. Leaving keys in a door or lying about.

    1st offence, 5 s.; 2nd offence, 10 s.; 3rd offence, suspension.

12. Sleeping while on duty, by night, suspension.

13. Omitting at the proper times to ring the signal or cell-bell, should there be one.

14. Speaking unnecessarily of the prison arrangements in the hearing of prisoners or in public.

15. Omitting to make the prescribed reports at the proper times, or to keep the prescribed lists, rolls, or accounts.

16. Carelessly searching or omitting to search a prisoner, and allowing him, or her, to retain any forbidden article or money.

17. Neglecting to report the wish of a prisoner to see a Member of the General Prisons Board, the Inspector, Governor, Chaplain, Medical Officer, Chief or Principal Warder or Matron.

18. Neglecting to extinguish any lights or fires at the times appointed.

    1st offence, 1 s.; 2nd offence, 2 s.; 3rd offence, 4 s.

19. Neglecting to have the lights, lamps, candles, &c., properly trimmed and burning at the times appointed.

20. Omitting to mark or pull the roll-tale at the appointed times.

21. Neglecting to answer a prisoner's call or bell.

22. Neglecting to examine the cell or other buildings under their charge, and to examine and search the wards, cells, bedding, &c.

23. Allowing tools or other materials, or any cleaning articles, to be lying about out of their appointed places.

24. Allowing dirt to accumulate in the wards, cells, yards, or passages, or other places under their charge.

25. Neglecting to attend to the cleanliness of the prisoners in their charge, or the necessary repairs of their clothing.

26. Omitting to report any injury done to the prison furniture or any marks or defacings on the walls, windows, partitions, or paint, or other portions of the prison under their charge or superintendence.

27. Allowing prisoners to leave the wards or cells improperly dressed.

28. Inattention when in charge of prisoners in the wards, or when at labour or exercise, &c.

29. Communicating with unauthorised persons in the prison or outside when in charge of prisoners.

30. Omitting to give notice in writing to the Governor, or appointed officer, previously to leaving the prison on leave of absence.

31. Allowing strangers to enter the wards, sheds, or exercising yards, when occupied by prisoners, unless by order of the General Prisons Board, the Governor, or other competent authority.

32. Appearing in or outside the prison improperly dressed, slovenly, unshaven, or unclean.

33. Appearing at any time, without permission, within the prison or beyond the prison walls, out of uniform.

34. Being absent from quarters, when resident, after the hour appointed at night without special leave.

35. Wrangling together, whether on duty or not, or in any way obstructing the duties of the prison.

36. Omitting to report without delay any irregularity or omission of duty on their own part or that of any officer, or servant, or a prisoner.

    1st offence, 1 s.; 2nd offence, 1 s. 6 d.; 3rd offence, 2 s.

37. Omitting when sick to send or deliver a medical certificate or notice to the Governor or Matron, or omitting when convalescent to report his or her return (in writing) before 10 o'clock on the day of such return.

    1st offence, 6 d.; 2nd offence, 1 s. 6 d.; 3rd offence, 3 s.

                       38. Omitting

38. Omitting to count the prisoners going to and returning from work or exercise, and at locking up and unlocking, or other appointed times.

39. Omitting at any time to withdraw from the halls, yards, shops, wards, or cells, such tools, implements, and articles as ought to be withdrawn.

40. Making unnecessary noise in or about the prison.

    1st offence, 1 s.; 2nd offence, 2 s.; 3rd offence, 4 s.

Cook.

41. Serving more or less than the prisoners' proper allowance of food.

42. Inattention to the cooking of the officers or prisoners' meals, or negligently spoiling the same.

43. Neglecting to keep such accounts of provisions, &c., as may be required of him or her, or immediately to report any deficiency in the quality of the provisions.

44. Omitting to prepare the meals at the appointed times, whether for officers or prisoners.

45. Neglecting to keep the kitchen, store-rooms, or other parts of the prison under his or her charge, together with the furniture and utensils therein, in clean condition and good order.

    1st offence, 1 s. 6 d.; 2nd offence, 3 s.; 3rd offence, 5 s.

Gate-Keeper.

46. Omitting to attend at the gate at the time appointed.

    1st offence, 1 s.; 2nd offence, 2 s.; 3rd offence, 3 s.

47. Allowing prisoners to pass the gate without being in charge of an officer of the prison, suspension.

All Subordinate Officers and Servants.

48. Disobedience or negligence with respect to any of the prison rules or regulations not here expressly mentioned, or to any order given by their superior officers or persons in authority connected with the prison.

    For each offence any sum not less than 6 d., nor exceeding 2 s. 6 d.; 2nd offence, double; 3rd offence, treble.

The repetition of an offence will not be deemed a second or third offence under this scale, unless occurring within six months of the previous offence. Any offence repeated beyond the third time will be specially reported for the consideration of the General Prisons Board, except cases of being late for duty, which will be specially reported whenever the Governor may consider it necessary.

Fines exceeding 6 s. and not exceeding 10 s. can be imposed by order of the Inspector.

A member of the General Prisons Board and Visiting Justices shall have the power to fine any subordinate officers for neglect or violation of duty; in no case to exceed one month's pay of the officer fined. If a greater punishment is required, a representation must be made to the Government with a view to the officer's being recommended for dismissal.

Their Excellencies the Lords Justices approve.

                (signed)   Thomas H. Burke.

13 June 1878.

THE GENERAL PRISONS (IRELAND) ACT, 1877.

RULES for the DIETARIES of the LOCAL PRISONS in IRELAND, subject to the General Prisons (Ireland) Act, 1877.

RULES for the DIETARIES of the LOCAL PRISONS in Ireland, as Approved 18th February 1884 and 17th January 1887.

The Terms to which the first three Classes of the above Diets are intended to be severally applied are those set forth in the following Table:—

TERM.	CLASS 1.	CLASS 2.	CLASS 3.
Three days and under	Whole term.	—	—
More than three days and not more than one month.	Three days	Remainder of term.	—
More than one month and not more than four months.	—	One month	Remainder of term.
More than four months	—	—	Whole term.

NOTE.—Two pints of buttermilk may be given as an equivalent for one pint of new milk. Bread may be given as an equivalent for stirabout, at the discretion of the medical officer, in the proportion of 5 oz. and 7½ oz. bread for 1 and 1½ pints meal respectively. In case of a Fast Day in the Roman Catholic Church, falling on any day other than Wednesday or Friday, the prisoners of that Class may be given 6½ oz. of each day the same diet as on Friday.

The word "Term" includes the period, or aggregate of the periods, during which a convicted prisoner is to be confined in custody, whether under one, or more than one, sentence.

Rules for the Dietaries of the Local Prisons in Ireland.

Ingredients and Instructions.

Bread	To be made with whole meal, which is to consist of all the produce of grinding the wheaten grain, with the exception of the coarser bran.
Soup	In every pint 4 oz. beef (or shoulder), cheek, neck, leg, or shin of beef; 4 oz. split peas; 3 oz. fresh vegetables; ½ oz. onions; pepper and salt.
Suet pudding	1½ oz. mutton suet, 6 oz. flour, and about 6½ oz. water to make 1 lb.
Stirabout	Equal parts of Indian meal and oatmeal, with salt. The Indian meal requires more cooking than the oatmeal. To make 1½ pints stirabout, boil ½ plain water, to which ½ oz. of salt should be added; stir in 3 oz. of Indian meal, and afterwards 3 oz. oatmeal; keep constantly stirring, and when the whole are cooked, the required quantity of 1½ pint stirabout will be produced.*
Cocoa	To every pint, ¾ oz. flaked or Admiralty cocoa. Governor; — For flaked cocoa, ¼ oz. molasses or sugar to the pint. For Admiralty cocoa, ¼ oz. molasses or sugar to the pint.
Meat liquor, or broth	The liquor in which the meat is cooked cut. Stirabout is to be thickened with ½ oz. flour, and flavoured with ½ oz. onions to each ration, with pepper and salt to taste.
Vegetable soup	Add to 1 gallon of boiling water ½ oz. pearl barley, 6 oz. oatmeal (blended in a little cold water), 2 lbs. of carrots peeled and sliced, 4 oz. of onions cut small, and pepper and salt to taste; when boiled for one hour the soup is fit for use. Parsnips or carrots may be substituted for turnips. The outer leaves of celery are the same as mentioned addition to that soup, and where celery is grown it would be well to add them in the proportion of ½ oz. to each gallon.
Tea	See instructions under Hospital Diet.

* This is the formula for oatmeal as in Class I., the quantities to be increased as per sign for stirabout as in Class 2.

Table of Substitutes for Cooked Irish Beef.

(All the Meats to be weighed without Bones).

	Cooked Beef or Mutton Preserved by Heat.	Bacon ; and Pork Barrels (with a signed after cooking).	Australian or other Foreign Beef Fresh and by Cook.;	Cooked Fresh Fish	Cooked Salt Meat.	Cooked Salt Fish.
	oz.		oz.	oz.	oz.	oz.
In lieu of 4 oz. cooked Irish beef	8	Bacon 6 oz. / Pork Barrels 1 oz.	4	6		13
In lieu of 5 oz. cooked Irish beef	3½	Bacon 7 oz. / Salt Barrels 2 oz.	5	4	4½	3

† The nutritive proportion of this meat are improved by further heating, and it should be served cold.
‡ Beef or Wicklow bacon, dealt in the gross state and disossessed ; or boiled bacon. Weighed after cooking.

Table of Substitutes for Potatoes.

(All weighed after Cooking).

	Cabbage or Turnip Tops.	Parsnips, Turnips, or Carrots.	Preserved (Liened) Potatoes.	Loaves.	Rice Steeped and Swelled.
	oz.	oz.	oz.	oz.	oz.
In lieu of 16 oz. potatoes	6	23	16	8	17
In lieu of 10 oz. potatoes	7	99	13	7	10
In lieu of 8 oz. potatoes	6	9	6	6	5
In lieu of 6 oz. potatoes	5	6	6	5	6

DIETS FOR ILL-CONDUCTED OR IDLE PRISONERS.

No. 1.—Bread and Water Diet.—Men and Women.

1 lb. Bread per Diem, with Water.

This diet to be limited, in the first place, to three days; after that, one of the under-mentioned diets, according to labour performed, for three days before its repetition, when it is again to be limited to three days, and a second interval on one of the undermentioned diets is to elapse before it is again enjoined. The entire period, including intervals, to which any single turn of this diet may be ordered, is not to exceed 15 days. No task of labour is to be enforced on any one of the nine days on which the bread and water constitute the sole food supplied to the prisoner.

No. 2.—Reformed Diet.

For Men and Women performing a Daily Task of any Labour not expressly defined as Hard Labour.

Breakfast	. . . .	Bread, 8 ounces
Dinner	. . . .	1 pint stirabout, containing 8 ounces meal, and 2 ounces Indian meal, with salt. Potatoes, 8 ounces.
Supper	. . . .	Bread, 8 ounces.

This diet to be limited, in the first place, to 11 days; after that, the diet of the class to which the prisoner belongs, for one week before its repetition, when it is to be limited to 14 days. The entire period, including the interval, for which any single turn of this diet may be ordered, is not to exceed 62 days.

No. 3.—For Men performing a Daily Task of Hard Labour.

Breakfast	Daily . . .	1½ pint stirabout, containing 3½ ounces oatmeal, and 3½ ounces Indian meal.
Dinner	Sunday . . .	1 pint meat soup with 4 ounces beef without bone. Potatoes, 16 ounces.
	Monday Tuesday Thursday Saturday	} Bread, 16 ounces. Vegetable soup 1 pint.
	Wednesday Friday	} Bread, 8 ounces. Potatoes, 16 ounces.
Supper	Daily . . .	Bread, 10 ounces. Cocoa, 1 pint.

This diet to be limited to 82 days; after that the diet Class 2 shall be resumed for 14 days, before its repetition. The governor shall have authority to direct this dietary for any period not exceeding 36 days.

HOSPITAL DIETS.—MEN AND WOMEN.

DIETS	PER DAY					
	Bread.	Cooked Mutton, without bone.	Pea Soup.	Rice Pudding.	Arrowroot, made with Milk.	Tea.
	oz.	oz.	oz.	oz.	oz.	oz.
Ordinary	16	8	20	8	—	—
Low	8	—	10*	—	10	16

* Additional to that in ordinary.

Hospital Diets—continued.

The following Articles may be ordered as Extras or Substitutes in the Quantities deemed necessary by the Medical Officer:

Ale.	Fruit.	Poultry.
Bacon.	Groats (or other vegetables).	Rice (ground).
Beef tea.	Ice.	Sago.
Biscuits.	Jam.	Spirit.
Butter.	Jelly.	Sauce.
Cake.	Lemonade.	Sugar.
Cocoa.	Milk.	Tea.
Coffee.	Porter.	Waters (mineral).
Corn flour.	Potatoes.	Wine.
Eggs.		

INSTRUCTIONS.

Rice Pudding — 2 ounces rice; 1 pint milk; 1 ounce sugar; 1 egg and nutmeg to produce 20 ounces.

Arrowroot — 1 ounce arrowroot; 1 pint milk; 1 ounce sugar, to produce 1 pint.

Beef tea — 16 ounces of the lean parts of the neck of the ox to 1 pint water.

Tea — ¼ ounce tea; ½ ounce sugar; 2 ounces milk, and water to make up ½ pint.

Cocoa — ½ ounce flaked or Admiralty cocoa to 1 pint water, sweetened with ½ ounce molasses or sugar for flaked cocoa, and ½ ounce molasses or sugar for Admiralty cocoa.

Lemonade — ½ ounce cream of tartar; ½ lemon (sliced); 2 ounces loaf sugar; water, 1½ pint. The water to be added hot to the other ingredients, and the whole to be allowed to stand till cold; then strain.

Mutton — To be meat or baked on four days in the week, and boiled on three days. On the days on which the mutton is boiled the meat liquor to be thickened with ½ ounce flour, and flavoured with ½ ounce onions per diet.

DIETARIES IN BRIDEWELLS.

Confined.			Convicted.			
Breakfast	Daily, Stout	8 oz.	Breakfast	Daily	Bread	8 oz.
					Tea or cocoa	1 pint.
					Or, at option of prisoner, oatmeal, constituting of 8¼ oz. oatmeal and 1¼ oz. fat, boiled, Meal	1½ pint.
					New milk	1 pint.
Dinner	Daily	Stirabout, consisting of 8 oz. Indian meal and 8 oz. oatmeal	1½ pint.	Dinner	Daily	Bread	16 oz.
						Milk*	1 pint.
Supper	Daily, Bread	8 oz.	Supper	Daily	Bread	8 oz.
					Tea or cocoa	1 pint.

* Milk to be given twice in each number.
For Regulations and Instructions, see page 32.

CONVICT PRISONS.

RULES FOR THE TREATMENT OF PRISONERS CONFINED IN CONVICT PRISONS IN IRELAND.

APPROVED BY THE LORD LIEUTENANT AND PRIVY COUNCIL.

GENERAL RULES FOR PRISONERS.

1. When prisoners are brought to the prison, notice of their arrival shall be given without delay, to the governor and medical officer; the officer first receiving them shall see that all the required documents are delivered with them; and no receipt in acknowledgment of their admission will be signed until these documents shall have been examined. Any omission or irregularity in the documents shall be reported immediately to the governor, and a note thereof made on the back of the receipt.

2. Prisoners, on arrival at the prison, shall be searched, and made to wash themselves thoroughly, under such general regulations as may be recommended by the medical officer, and approved of by the superior authorities of the prison. They shall then be examined by the medical officer, and, when required, be kept separate until certified by him to be fit to be received among the other prisoners, or removed, if necessary, to the infirmary. Any instance of a prisoner being found medically unfit to have been sent to the prison will be immediately reported, with the particulars in writing, to the governor by the medical officer, in order that the circumstances may be reported without delay to the General Prisons Board for the information of the Lord Lieutenant. Prisoners shall put on the prison dress, and, if necessary, have their hair cut short.

3. The governor shall cause to be inserted in a book entitled "The Prisoners' Property Book," an entry (to be signed by the prisoner and attested by an officer of the prison) of any money, or other property delivered with or found upon the prisoner on his admission, or that may be sent to him afterwards, which money or other property the steward shall take into his possession, to be accounted for or returned to such prisoner when discharged from the prison; but any such money, or other property, may, at any time during the prisoner's confinement, be delivered to his friends, with the approbation of the governor, under an authority signed by the prisoner, and attested by the chaplain. Any prohibited articles introduced by prisoners, such as tobacco, or articles of food not authorised to be used in the prison, will be destroyed; money so attempted to be introduced, or that may be found on a prisoner or secreted by or for him, shall be forfeited, and carried to the credit of the public. Any money or articles (not prohibited) sent to a prisoner may be received by the governor but a deposit for the use of each prisoner, to be delivered to him or remitted for upon his discharge. All property kept for any prisoner shall be made up into parcels, to be docketed with the name of the prisoner to whom they belong, and shall be kept in a distinct place to be appropriated to that purpose in the steward's store.

A ticket shall be given to each convict, as soon as possible after his reception into the prison, specifying whether any or what money or other property has been received by the governor on his account. This ticket shall be signed by the storekeeper and countersigned by the governor.

4. After prisoners are received at the prison, the Abstract of the Rules relating to the conduct and treatment of prisoners, as well as the notice which specially explains the direct effect of each prisoner's conduct on his present and future prospects, shall be read over to them by the appointed officer, and proper means will afterwards be taken by the governor for making them acquainted with the purport and effect of such rules. A copy of this Abstract and the "Notice" shall be suspended in each division of the prison, and in such other places occupied by the prisoners as may appear desirable.

5. No prisoner shall disobey the orders of the governor or any other officer, or treat any of the officers or servants of the prison, or any person who may visit the prison, or may be employed therein, or on the Public Works, with disrespect; or be idle or negligent in his work, or absent himself, without leave, from Divine Service or Prayers, or behave irreverently thereat; or be guilty of swearing or any indecent or immoral expression or actions; or of any assault, quarrel, or provoking or abusive language or curses, or hold intercourse with any other prisoner, except as authorised by the prison Rules;

Rules, or cause annoyance or disturbance by singing, whistling, or making unnecessary noise; or pass, or attempt to pass, without permission, out of his cell, or beyond the bounds of the ward or other place to which he may belong; or when at work, go without leave beyond the limits assigned for such work, or be idle at his work; or disfigure the walls or other parts of the prison by writing on them or otherwise; or deface, mutilate, destroy, or pull down any paper or order hung up by authority in or about any part of the prison; or wilfully injure any bedding or other article, or commit any nuisance; or have in his cell or possession any article not furnished by the Establishment, or allowed to be in the possession of a prisoner; or shall give, or lend to, or borrow from, any other prisoner, any food, book, or other article without leave; or refuse or neglect to conform to the Rules, Regulations, or Orders of the prison, or otherwise offend.

6. The governor may examine any persons touching such offences, and may order any prisoner so offending to be punished by being closely or otherwise confined in a dark or light cell, or by being fed on bread and water only, or by such punishments, for any term not exceeding three days; or by removal to a lower class; or by suspension for a time without actual removal of the privileges of his class; or, in case of necessity, he may place a prisoner in irons.

If any prisoner be guilty of an offence for which the punishment hereinbefore authorised to be inflicted shall be deemed by the governor to be insufficient, on account of the enormity of the offence, or the repetition thereof, the governor shall, without loss of time, report the same to the General Prisons Board, who are hereby empowered to punish such prisoner in such manner as is authorised by law.

7. The governor shall have authority to place any prisoner in separate confinement in the cells provided for the purpose, for a period not exceeding 28 days; recording each case in which he may consider it necessary to exercise this discretionary power in his Journal. If a longer period of separation should be deemed by him to be desirable, he will apply to the General Prisons Board, who will give such directions thereupon as they may deem expedient.

8. Every prisoner in separate confinement shall be furnished with the means of employment, and moral and religious instruction. He shall be supplied with suitable books, and have as much exercise in the open air as the governor shall direct, or the medical officer may deem necessary for his health. He shall be visited daily by the governor, chaplain, and medical officer, and shall attend Divine Service and daily Prayers, unless special directions, under particular circumstances, should be given.

9. Every prisoner shall usually be confined at night in a small cell, and shall be employed, unless prevented by sickness, in such work as the governor shall appoint, every day, except Sundays; and the holydays of the Church to which the prisoner belongs, the hours of work in each day not to exceed twelve, exclusive of the time allowed for meals. No prisoner shall be employed in the discipline of the prison, or in the service of any officer or servant thereof.

10. Prisoners shall be selected, under the governor's directions, to attend to the cleanliness of the different parts of the prison, but always under the inspection of the warders or other officers or servants of the prison. Prisoners shall also be selected by the governor to assist in the cook-house and baking, where they shall be under the charge of the baker and cook of the prison, or other person appointed to take charge of them.

11. On Sundays, the cleaning shall be confined to what is strictly necessary for the order of the prison. The prisoners shall attend Divine Service, take such exercise in the open air as may be ordered by the governor or medical officer, and read and receive instruction under the superintendence of the chaplains on the days appointed by the Church to which the prisoner belongs. On week days the prisoner shall receive such school instruction as may from time to time be directed.

12. The prisoners shall wash their hands and faces at such hours, and as often daily as may be directed, and shall shave every second day at the appointed hours; they shall wash their feet or bathe once a week, as may be directed by the medical officer, and shall be allowed clean linen and clean towels once a week, and clean sheets once a month. Their hair shall be cut when required, so as to keep it quite clean at all times. They shall be required to keep their cells, and everything therein, constantly neat and clean, and all articles in their proper places.

The bedding is to be frequently removed from the cells; to be aired under such regulations as may from time to time be established.

13. Prisoners shall not, during the period of their confinement, be permitted to see their friends unless by order in writing, signed by the governor or other superior authority. The interview between the prisoners and their friends can only take place in the presence of an officer of the prison, for the space of 20 minutes, and in the rooms appropriated for that purpose, except in special cases to be determined at the discretion of the governor. All letters to or from prisoners shall be inspected by the governor and chaplain,

Letters to and from prisoners to be inspected.

chaplain, who shall forward or keep back the same, according to the nature of their contents; recording in their journals the reasons for withholding any letters. Letters to prisoners shall be brought to the governor in the first instance, and be forwarded by him to the chaplain for delivery; those from prisoners shall pass through the chaplain to the governor.

Times of writing and of receiving letters or visits.

14. Every prisoner may, upon reception, write one letter. The privilege afterwards of writing a letter or receiving a letter or visit shall be at intervals of three months, the first exercise of such privilege to take place three months after the prisoner's reception, or being permitted to write a letter as above, and the succeeding intervals to be reckoned from the last letter or visit for the time being. Letters disapproved of will be suppressed, and the privilege may thus have forfeited, if the governor judges the forfeiture necessary. In case of misconduct, the privilege shall be postponed or forfeited at the discretion of the governor or other superior authority, the governor recording in his journal all instances in which he may exercise the discretion. Events of importance to prisoners may be communicated to them at any other period by the governor.

The foregoing general rule shall be subject to the special rules as to letters and visits for each class.

Relaxation of rules as to letters and visits.

Special applications under particular circumstances from prisoners of the first class, for relaxation of this rule as to letters and visits, will be favourably considered by the governor and chaplain, under such regulations as may from time to time be established.

Convicts escaping or breaking prison.

Attempting to escape or break prison.

15. Any prisoner who at any time shall break prison, or who, while being conveyed to any convict prison, shall escape from the person or persons having the lawful custody of such prisoner, shall be punished by an addition, not exceeding two years, to the term of his sentence; and any prisoner who at any time shall attempt to break prison, or who shall forcibly break out of his cell, or make any breach therein with intent to escape therefrom, or shall escape or attempt to escape when at work outside the prison, shall be punished by an addition, not exceeding one year, to the term of his imprisonment.

Rules applicable to MALE PRISONERS only.

Corporal punishment.

The following offences committed by adult male prisoners (that is, prisoners of 18 years of age and upwards) will render them liable to corporal punishment:

1st. Mutiny or open incitement to mutiny in a prison; personal violence to any officer or servant of the prison, or to a fellow prisoner, or threats of such violence; grossly offensive or abusive language to any officer or servant of the prison.

2nd. Wilfully or wantonly breaking the prison windows, or otherwise destroying the prison property.

3rd. When under punishment in a dark, refractory, or ordinary cell, wilfully making a disturbance tending to interrupt the order and discipline of the prison, and any other act of gross misconduct or insubordination requiring to be suppressed by extraordinary means.

4th. Corporal punishment shall in no case be awarded until after the inquiry upon oath, and in the presence of the prisoner, into the circumstances of the case. Full particulars of the inquiry shall, in each case, be entered in the Minute Book of the General Prisons Board.

5th. The order for the punishment shall be entered in the Order Book of the General Prisons Board, and the number of lashes to be inflicted shall, in all cases, be stated in such order.

6th. In no case of corporal punishment shall the number of lashes inflicted on an adult prisoner exceed 36, or on a juvenile prisoner 18.

7th. Corporal punishment, in the case of adult prisoners, to be inflicted with a "cat" or birch, and, in the case of juvenile prisoners, with a birch rod; the instruments, in both instances, to be previously approved by the General Prisons Board.

8th. The governor shall attend all corporal punishments, and shall enter in his journal the day and hour at which the punishment is inflicted, the number of lashes given, and any orders which he or the medical officer may give on the occasion.

9th. The

9th. The medical officer shall have power to remit any portion of the number of lashes awarded.

10th. The medical officer shall attend all corporal punishments, and his instructions thereon, for preventing injury to health, shall be obeyed.

11th. In every case, before corporal punishment is inflicted, the medical officer shall ascertain that the prisoner is in a fit state of health to undergo punishment.

12th. In the case of juvenile prisoners, corporal punishment may be inflicted for any repeated offence against the rules of the prison, or for any greater offence than the governor is otherwise empowered adequately to punish.

MISCELLANEOUS RULES.

1. No stranger, except the Judges of the High Court of Justice, and such persons as may come with them, or unless accompanied by the governor, shall be admitted to see any part of the prison or premises in the occupation of the prisoners, unless by an order from the Lord Lieutenant. Persons admitted to see the prison are expected to give their names and address, to be inserted in a book to be kept for that purpose by the governor; and they are desired to abstain from any conversation, in the hearing of the prisoners, respecting the crimes for which they were sent to the prison. *[margin: Strangers not permitted to see the prison unless by order of the Lord Lieutenant.]*

2. The fire-engines and fire-plugs shall be kept in constant readiness for use, and worked periodically, to keep them in proper order, and examine the officers to direct the prisoners how to use them with proper effect. The utmost care shall be taken by every officer or servant of the prison to guard against accidents by fire, from the lights, furnaces, &c., in and about the prison. It is their duty immediately to report any danger of such accidents that they may observe in any part of the establishment, and to use all possible means to prevent them. No lights or fires are to be left burning unnecessarily, or unattended to, in any part of the prison. No light is at any time to be carried about the prison, unless it is enclosed in a lantern; and each officer coming on duty during the night is to examine all parts of the prison to see that they are safe from fire. *[margin: Accidents from fire to be carefully guarded against.]*

In case of a fire occurring in any building occupied by prisoners or contiguous thereto, safety to life is the main object to be attended to in the first instance; the secure custody of the prisoners and steps for extinguishing the fire will be the next consideration. *[margin: Orders to be observed in case of fire.]*

3. No dogs (except for security) shall be kept in the prison. *[margin: Dogs not to be kept.]*

4. No trees shall be allowed to grow against the outer walls, and no rubbish or other article shall be laid against them. *[margin: Rubbish, &c.]*

5. No books shall be permitted for the use of prisoners, except such as are specified in lists, to be from time to time sanctioned by proper authority. *[margin: Books for the use of prisoners.]*

6. All convicts may be photographed before release for the purpose of identification. The man's name, offence, date of conviction and discharge and sentence should be inserted on the photograph.

SYSTEM of CLASSIFICATION to be adopted for all Male Convicts undergoing their first Period of Probation under their Sentences on the 1st February 1861, and for all Male Convicts received into Convict Prisons after that date, and for all Male Convicts who, by reason of Misconduct, have been or may hereafter be ordered by the General Prisons Board to be placed under this System.

1. All stages and classes in operation previous to 1st February 1861, to be abolished for all such convicts.

2. A convict during the term of his imprisonment will be required to pass through the following classes, viz.:—

Probation class, one year, during which he must earn on public works 720 marks . . . . } *[margin: Minimum period with good conduct and industry.]*
Third class, one year, during which he must earn on public works 2,920 marks . . . . }
Second class, one year, during which he must earn 2,920 marks)

After which he will be eligible for promotion to the 1st class.

3. Every convict is thus required to remain in the probation class for a minimum period of one year, reckoned from the date of conviction, of which nine months will be passed in separate confinement.

E 4 4. If

4. If his conduct and industry are good he will then be promoted to the 3rd class, and so on to the 2nd, remaining in each a minimum period of one year.

. 5. Prisoners detained in separate confinement for misconduct cannot be promoted to the 3rd class until three months after they have become eligible for removal to public works.

6. The remainder of the term of his imprisonment will be spent in the 1st class, unless he is promoted to the special class, or Intermediate Class, or degraded to any lower class.

7. These classes will be kept quite separate from each other in the prison.

8. Convicts in the Probation Class will be subjoined, while undergoing separate confinement, to the special rules and regulations approved of for that class. On removal to public works they will continue in the Probation Class until they have completed twelve months, reckoning from the date of conviction, with good conduct.
Prisoners in the Probation Class will wear the ordinary convicts' dress without facings.

9. Prisoners in this class on the public works will be allowed no gratuity, nor to receive visits, nor to receive or write letters, except on remission from separate confinement; they will be allowed one period of exercise on Sunday.

10. If their conduct and industry are either bad or indifferent, either in separate confinement or after their removal to public works, they will be detained in the Probation Class until they have earned an additional number of marks to that allotted to the period to be passed in probation.

11. Prisoners in the 3rd Class will wear the ordinary grey convicts' dress with black facings.
They will be allowed:

1st. To receive a gratuity of 10s., being at the rate of 1s. per month for 12 months, to be earned by marks during the time spent in this class, and if their conduct shows that they deserve it.

2nd. To receive a visit of 20 minutes' duration, once in six months, at such time as the Governor approves, care being taken that the stipulated number is not exceeded, and both to receive and write a letter once in six months, provided their conduct in that class has been good for at least two previous consecutive months.

12. Prisoners in the 2nd Class will wear the ordinary grey convicts' dress with yellow facings.
They will be allowed:

1st. To receive a visit of 30 minutes' duration, and both to receive and write a letter once in four months.

2nd. To receive a gratuity of 15s., calculated at 1s. 6d. per month for 12 months, to be earned by marks during the time spent in this class, and if their conduct shows that they deserve it.

3rd. To have two periods of exercise during Sundays.

13. Prisoners in the 1st Class will wear the ordinary grey convicts' dress with blue facings.
They will be allowed:

1st. To receive a visit of half an hour, and both to receive and write a letter once in three months.

2nd. Prisoners in this class will be allowed a gratuity of 20s., being at the rate of 2s. 6d. per month for 16 months, to be earned by marks until they have earned 3l. altogether.

3rd. To be eligible, if their conduct and industry are good, and the total gratuity of 3l. is earned, and if they are not promoted to the Intermediate Class, to be recommended on discharge for a further gratuity not exceeding 3l.

4th. To be allowed three periods of exercise on Sundays.

14. No convict is to be promoted to the 1st Class until he can read and write, except in special cases which must be approved of by the General Prisons Board.

15. Special Class.— No convict is to be admitted into the Special Class till he is within 12 months of his release, and has passed through the First Class with exemplary conduct. Convicts in the Special Class will wear a blue dress.

They will be allowed:

1st. To be eligible to be recommended for an extra remission, not exceeding one week.

2nd. To

2nd. To be eligible for appointments of trust

3rd. To be eligible, if not promoted to the Intermediate Class, for the extra gratuity of 3£ on discharge, which may be handed to a Prisoners' Aid Society.

4th. To receive a visit of half an hour, and to receive and write a letter once in two months.

16. Intermediate Class.
Convicts who are considered eligible for the Intermediate Class are permitted to pass the latter portion of their sentence in that Class before release on licence.
Convicts in the Intermediate Class will wear the dress of the Special Class with I. badge.

17. The period to be passed in this class varies according to the prisoner's sentence; 9½ months being the period under a five years' sentence, and a month additional being allowed for every additional year of sentence.

18. No convict will be considered eligible for the Intermediate Class till he is in the Special Class, or, if under five years' sentence, in the 1st class, and has earned the required number of marks under his sentence.

19. The following classes of convicts are ineligible for the Intermediate Class:— Convicts whose crimes or previous circumstances in life preclude them from being treated in the ordinary manner; those who have passed on a former occasion through the Intermediate Class or an Intermediate Prison, those who are imbecile or unfit for labour, and those who are guilty of heinous offences.

20. There may also be other exceptional cases where the convicts concerned will be adjudged ineligible for the Intermediate Class.

21. Convicts under sentence of five years, who cannot attain the special class, and are not eligible for the Intermediate Class, may be recommended for an extra gratuity of 2£, which may be handed to a Prisoners' Aid Society, on discharge; provided they have not forfeited more than two marks for rueness, and have passed nine months in the 1st class with exemplary conduct.

22. All prisoners will wear a badge on the sleeve of their jacket, which will denote their register number and sentence; and also their register number on their cap.

23. For practical purposes in calculating the gratuities, the following scale may be adopted:—

In the 3rd class, 10 marks are equal to .   .   . 1 d.
In the 2nd class, 10 marks are equal to .   .   . 1½ d.
In the 1st class, 10 marks are equal to .   .   . 2½ d.

24. Convicts sentenced to penal class or cross irons, or to wear the parti-coloured or distinctive dress while under such punishment, to be placed in the probation class; after which they will return to their original class, unless the sentence specifies to the contrary.

25. Convicts removed to public works from special probation in separate confinement will go through the classes in the same way as convicts then removed from separate confinement.

REGULATIONS.—MARK SYSTEM.

1. The time which every convict, under sentence of penal servitude, must henceforth pass in prison will be represented by a certain number of marks which he must earn by actual labour performed before he can be discharged.

2. No remission will be granted for conduct. It is only on condition of good conduct and strict obedience that convicts are allowed to earn by their industry a remission of a portion of their sentences.

3. If, therefore, their conduct is indifferent, or bad, they will be liable to be fined a certain number of marks, according to the nature and degree of the offence, and will thus forfeit, by misconduct, the remission they may have earned by their industry.

4. The scale of marks is:—
Eight marks per diem for steady hard labour and the full performance of their allotted task.
Seven marks per diem for a less degree of industry.
Six marks per diem for a fair but moderate day's work.

5. No remission is granted for the period passed in separate confinement, which is fixed at nine months; a convict's marks are therefore to be calculated at the rate of six per diem, as commencing nine months from the date of conviction, and any forfeiture of them

time incurred in separate confinement is to be added to his marks at the rate of six for every day forfeited; but if he is detained through no fault of his own in a separate prison above nine months from date of sentence, he will be credited with eight marks per diem for the days he is so detained. After 12 months he is to be classed for labour, and credited with marks according to his labour class, as if on public works.

6. If by his industry on public works the convict gains eight marks per diem, and does not forfeit any for misconduct, he earns the full remission of one-fourth allowed by the Lord Lieutenant.

7. The scale of remission to every convict is to be one-fourth of his period on public works.

No expectation of release from prison can be held out to convicts sentenced to penal servitude for life after 12th July 1884, until they have completed 20 years, except in cases where sentence of death was not recorded, which cases should be submitted for consideration at the end of 15 years, or except there are other special circumstances affecting the cases. Every case submitted for consideration must be taken on its own merits.

8. When a convict is sentenced to forfeiture of time, a number of marks equal to the number of days forfeited, multiplied by six, is to be added to the whole number of marks he has to earn; as he can by industry earn eight, he may thereby gain a remission of one-fourth of such forfeiture.

9. When a convict is sentenced to be degraded for a certain time to a lower class, he must remain therein until he has earned the full number of marks for that time, viz., the whole number of days multiplied by eight; such number of marks is not, however, to be added to the original number he has to earn for remission, but it represents the number of marks he must earn before he can return to his original class, unless the sentence specifies to the contrary.

10. Convicts in the light labour class to be credited only with six or seven marks, according to their character and industry, unless specially otherwise ordered by the General Prisons Board.

11. Convicts sentenced to separate confinement or penal class, or while undergoing second probation, to be credited only with six marks per diem during that period.

12. Convicts in hospital to be credited only with six marks per diem, which may be increased by special recommendation of the Governor to the General Prisons Board.

13. The record of marks to be kept by the Infirmary Principal Warder, and submitted to the Medical Officer, who will make such recommendation as he sees fit to the Governor.

14. On Sunday marks must be allotted for conduct alone on that day.

15. Any prisoner reported for idleness or misconduct at school will be liable, in addition to any other punishment, to be fined a number of marks proportionate to his offence.

16. Convicts who, by their inattention, do not profit by the instruction given them, and are found unable to read and write on emerging from the third class, will forfeit their gratuity, which cannot be restored to them until they can do so.

17. The power of the Governor to fine convicts for remission is limited to the equivalent in marks of their present power of forfeiture of time, viz., from one to 14 days, the equivalent being from six to 84 marks; and his power as to degradation of class is limited to three months, represented by 780 marks, which must be earned before the convict can regain his class, but which are not to be added to the total amount he has to earn for remission.

18. Reconvicted men will be placed in the same scale of remission as other convicts, and if their conduct is meritorious their cases will be submitted for favourable consideration at the same period as other convicts; but they will be more severely dealt with than other convicts if they misconduct themselves.

Convicts, however, who are reconvicted during the existence of their licenses, will, in addition to their minimum term of second sentence, be required to serve the whole of the remission they were allowed when going on license. License holders reconvicted a third time, i.e., twice reconvicted while on license, get no remission.

19. Convicts who by their misconduct forfeit the whole of their remission will be liable to be kept in separate confinement during the last six months of their sentence.

SYSTEM of CLASSIFICATION to be adopted for all Female Convicts who were on 1st Febuary 1861 undergoing their first period of Probation under their Sentences of Penal Servitude, and for all Female Convicts received into a Convict Prison after that date; and for all Female Convicts who, by reason of Misconduct, have been or may hereafter be ordered by the General Prison Board to be placed under this System.

1st. All stages and classes in operation previous to 1st February 1861, to be abolished for all such convicts.

2nd. A convict during the term of her imprisonment will be required to pass through the following classes, viz.—

Probation class, 9 months, during which she must earn 1,620 marks by good conduct and actual work performed . . . .

3rd class, 9 months, during which she must earn 1,620 marks as above . . . .

2nd class, 9 months (unless removed to a refuge under a 5 years' sentence before the completion of this period), during which she must earn 1,620 marks as above . . . .

} Minimum period with good conduct and industry.

After which she will be eligible for promotion to the 1st class.

It will be seen that no woman (with the exception made above) can be recommended for discharge, until she is in the 1st class.

3rd. Every convict is thus required to remain in the Probation Class for a minimum period of nine months, reckoned from the date of conviction.

4th. Prisoners detained in the Probation Class for misconduct cannot be promoted to the 3rd class until they have earned the additional number of marks forfeited by their misconduct.

5th. If her conduct and industry are good she will be promoted to the 3rd class, and so on to the 2nd, remaining in each a minimum period of nine months.

6th. The remainder of the term of her imprisonment will be spent in the 1st class, unless she is degraded to any lower class.

7th. Three classes will be kept quite separate from each other in the prison.

8th. Convicts in the Probation Class will be subjected while undergoing confinement to the Special Rules and Regulations approved of for that class. They will continue in the Probation Class until they have completed nine months, reckoning from the date of conviction with good conduct.
Prisoners in the Probation Class will wear the ordinary brown serge dress.

9th. Prisoners in this class will be allowed no gratuity, nor to receive visits or write letters, except one letter on reception from separate confinement; they will be allowed one period of exercise on Sunday.
The strictest silence will be enforced with prisoners in this class on all occasions.

10th. If their conduct and industry are either bad or indifferent, either in separate confinement or after their release therefrom, they will be detained in the Probation Class until they have earned an additional number of marks, to that allotted to the period to be passed in probation.

11th. On leaving the Probation Class the prisoners will be received into the 3rd class. The strictest silence to be enforced on all occasions on prisoners received into this class. Prisoners in this class will wear the ordinary brown serge dress and will wear No. 3 badge.

They will be allowed—

1st. To receive a gratuity of 18s., being at the rate of 2s. per month, for nine months, to be earned by marks during the time spent in this class, and if their conduct shows that they deserve it.

2nd. To receive a visit of 20 minutes' duration once in six months, at such time as the lady superintendent approves, care being taken that the stipulated number is not exceeded, and both to receive and write a letter once in three months, provided their conduct in that class has been good for at least two previous consecutive months.

3rd. They will be allowed one period of exercise on Sundays.

12th. Prisoners whose conduct has been exemplary in the 3rd class for a period of nine months will be promoted to the 2nd class; they will wear the green serge dress and No. 2 badge, and will be in association.

They will be allowed—

    1st. To receive a visit of 20 minutes' duration every four months, and both to receive and write a letter once in three months.

    2nd. To receive a gratuity of 18 s., calculated at 2 s. per month for nine months, to be earned by marks during the time spent in this class and if their conduct shows that they deserve it.

    3rd. To have two periods of exercise on Sundays.

13th. Prisoners whose conduct has been exemplary in the 2nd class for a period of nine months will be promoted to the first class. They will wear a dark blue serge dress, and No. 1 badge. In this class they will be in association.

They will be allowed—

    1st. To receive a visit of half an hour every three months, and both to receive and write a letter once in two months.

    2nd. Prisoners in this class will be allowed a gratuity of 2 l. 4 s., being at the rate of 4 s. per month to be earned by marks until they have earned 4 l. altogether.

    3rd. To be eligible, if their conduct and industry are good, and if special circumstances should render it desirable, to be recommended on discharge for a further gratuity not exceeding 2 l.

    4th. To be allowed two periods of exercise on Sundays, and half an hour's additional exercise every day.

14th. The 1st, 2nd, and 3rd classes will respectively be distinguished by badges marked No. 1, No. 2, and No. 3.

15th. The superintendent, with the sanction of the General Prisons Board, has the power to degrade a prisoner for the commission of an offence, from the 1st class to the 2nd class, or to the 3rd class or probation class, and every prisoner so degraded from a class will necessarily forfeit any advantage for which she may have been recommended while in that class.

16th. A prisoner who has been degraded to a lower class cannot regain her position until by her good conduct and industry she has earned the number of marks which represent the time for which she is sentenced to be reduced. The number of days for which she is sentenced being multiplied by four, will give the full time she has to serve in the class to which she is reduced.

17th. Gratuities will be credited to prisoners in the 1st, and 2nd, and 3rd classes, according to their industry, and the work they perform, and not exceeding 10 s. in the 3rd class, 16 s. in the 2nd class, and 2 l. 4 s. in the 1st class.

18th. This amount will be paid to the prisoners on their discharge, or laid out for their benefit at the discretion of the General Prisons Board, and under such regulations as the Lord Lieutenant may from time to time sanction.

19th. The cases of prisoners of advanced age or who are invalids, or who have infants, or who, from any other circumstances, may be unable to perform work, when in the 1st and 2nd classes, will be specially considered, with a view to some small gratuity being credited to them, provided their conduct be in all respects satisfactory.

20th. Every prisoner may upon exception write and receive one letter. The privilege afterwards of writing or receiving a letter shall be at intervals of three months in the 3rd and 2nd classes, and a visit every six months in the 3rd class, and every four months in the 2nd class; the first exercise of such privilege to take place at the discretion of the lady superintendent, or being permitted to write a letter as above, and the succeeding intervals to be reckoned from the last letter for the time being.

21st. First class prisoners to be allowed to write and receive letters at intervals of two months, and a visit every three months for half an hour. Letters disapproved of will be suppressed, and the privilege for that turn forfeited, if the superintendent judge the forfeiture necessary. In case of misconduct, the privilege shall be postponed, if forfeited, at the discretion of the superintendent, or other superior authority; the superintendent recording in her journal all instances in which she may exercise this discretion. All letters to or from prisoners shall be inspected by persons appointed for that purpose, and shall be forwarded or kept back according to the nature of their contents. Events of importance to prisoners may be communicated to them at any other period by the superintendent.

22nd. Convicts in the light labour class to be credited only with four or five marks, according to their character and industry, unless specially otherwise ordered by the General Prisons Board.

23rd. Convicts released from 2nd probation, in separate confinement, will go through the classes in the same way as convicts first received from separate confinement.

24th. Convicts

24th. Convicts in hospital to be credited only with four marks per diem, which may be increased by special recommendation of the lady superintendent to the General Prisons Board.

25th. The record of marks to be kept by the infirmary principal matron, and submitted to the medical officer, who will make such recommendation as he sees fit to the lady superintendent.

26th. The scale of marks is —

Six marks per diem for steady hard labour and the full performance of their allotted task.

Five marks per diem for a less degree of industry.

Four marks per diem for a fair but moderate day's work.

27th. The following qualifications are necessary to render a female convict eligible for a refuge :—

1st. She must be in the 1st class, except her sentence is one of five years, in which case she may become eligible for the refuge while in the 2nd class. Women who fail to obtain 1st class only from being unable to read and write, may, on special leave by the General Prisons Board, be presented for the purpose of being eligible for the refuge.

2nd. Her conduct and industry must be good.

3rd. Her health must be good, and she must be physically capable of earning a livelihood.

4th. She must not have more than eleven months' time to serve before becoming due for discharge on licence, or expiration of sentence.

5th. No convict who has been at a refuge before will be sent to one again without special sanction from the General Prisons Board; and no convict will be sent to a refuge who has had this privilege twice under former sentences.

6th. She must not have been guilty of violent and insubordinate conduct within six months. If she should have been, she should be degraded to a lower class.

7th. Previous to any convict becoming due to go to a refuge who was convicted of murder or violent assault, or whose crime or character is remarkable or notorious, the attention of the General Prisons Board should be specially called to the case, in order that they may address a communication to the manager of the refuge to ascertain whether she ought to be her sending to the refuge.

The foregoing rules were approved by the Lord Lieutenant and Privy Council by Orders dated 29th August 1883 and 30th December 1886.

RULES to be Observed in MOUNTJOY MALE PRISON.

By the General Prisons (Ireland) Act, 1877, 40 & 41 Vict. c. 49, sec. 9, all Powers, &c., vested in "the Directors of Convict Prisons," were transferred to "the General Prisons Board."

CONTENTS

GENERAL RULE FOR ALL PRISON OFFICERS, WHETHER SUPERIOR OR SUBORDINATE.

No prison officer (the governor alone excepted) shall, at any time or in any way, communicate with the friends of any prisoner, or communicate to any prisoner any information he may at any time learn respecting their friends. Any breach of this rule will be at once reported to the directors, and if proved, will be visited with immediate dismissal.

GENERAL RULE FOR EACH SUPERIOR OFFICER.*

Any breach of rules or improper treatment of officers or of prisoners on the part of any prison officers must be reported by him, in writing to a director, the inspector, or the governor, within 48 hours after such has come to his knowledge. This rule, however, would not exempt a superior officer from reporting, with as little delay as possible, any breach of rules, &c., which required immediate attention.

THE GOVERNOR.

1. The governor shall exercise no occupation or calling but that of governor of the prison. He shall reside at the prison, and shall not be absent from it for a night without permission, in writing, from a director; but if absent without leave for a night, from unavoidable necessity, he shall state the fact, and the cause of it in his journal. He shall also enter his leave of absence, with the authority for it, in his journal. Before leaving the prison at any time he shall give over the charge of it to the chief warder, or such other officer as a director may approve.

2. He shall have special superintendence over the prison and prisoners, and shall give his best attention to the application of their labour and the maintenance of discipline, visiting frequently each day all prisoners working in association. He shall make himself acquainted with the provisions of the several Acts of Parliament relating to prisons and with the prison rules, and shall adhere to them himself. He shall require obedience to the rules from the officers and servants of the prison, and from the military guard and sentries appointed for the security of the prison, and shall strictly enforce it on the prisoners. He shall observe the conduct of his subordinate officers, and require from each of them the due execution of their duties, as laid down by the rules; restricting them entirely to the performance of such duties, and not permitting any of them to be employed in any menial or private capacity, either for himself or for any other officer of the prison. He may authorise certain prisoners to be employed in the service of the prison, but not in its discipline, nor in his own private service or that of any of the officers.

3. He shall attend to the employment and industrial training of the prisoners, and assist with his influence and authority the exertions of the chaplains for their reformation, communicating freely and confidentially with them on subjects having reference to that object.

4. He

4. He shall exercise his authority with firmness, temper, and humanity; abstain from all irritating language, and shall not strike a prisoner. He shall bear in mind that the object of his duties, and of those of all officers and servants under his direction is not only to give full effect to the sentence awarded to the convicts during their period of confinement, but also to instil into their minds moral and religious principles, and induce in them practical habits of industry, regularity, and good conduct. With this view, while enforcing strict observance of the rules regarding labour and discipline, the governor will be careful to encourage every effort at amendment on the part of the prisoners, and will require all officers and servants of the prison, in their several capacities, to do the same. *(Treatment of the prisoners.)*

5. He, or the chief warder, shall attend Divine service in the prison, whenever it is performed, inserting in his journal any omission, and the cause thereof; he shall see that the subordinate officers and prisoners attend such service, unless prevented by illness, or excused by leave of absence, or by prison regulations; he shall deliver or cause to be delivered to the chaplains lists of prisoners absent from Divine Service, with a statement of the causes of their absence; and all such lists shall be signed by the governor or the chief warder. *(To attend Divine Service.)*

6. He shall cause an abstract of such of the rules as relate to the treatment and conduct of prisoners, and of the notices which specially explain the effect of each prisoner's conduct on his present and future prospects (printed in legible characters), to be fixed up in each cell of the prison; and he shall read, or cause to be read, such abstracts, at least once in every month to the prisoners, making a special entry thereof in his journal; or, in the event of this duty being omitted, stating the reason thereof. He shall take an early opportunity of seeing all prisoners after their admission, and shall satisfy himself that they understand the rules and regulations to which they are required to conform. *(Rules relating to prisoners to be fixed up in new prisoners places.)*

In the event of any prisoner's being received without the prescribed certificate and information from the prison from which he has been transferred, the governor shall apply for the necessary particulars, and in the event of his not being able to procure a satisfactory answer to such application, he shall immediately report the circumstance to the director. *(To apply for information, if not received with a prisoner.)*

7. He shall on all occasions be ready to receive and investigate any complaint, and attend to any application from an officer or prisoner; and he shall see daily any officer or prisoner who may request that he shall do so. *(Complaints from officers or prisoners.)*

8. He shall visit and inspect daily the wards, cells, yards, and divisions of the prison; also the kitchen and the workshops, and see all the prisoners once at least in every 24 hours, and see that they are industrious, and that all orders respecting the application of labour are duly enforced. He shall at least thrice during the week go through the prison at an uncertain hour of the night; which visit, with the hour and state of the prison at the time, he shall record in his journal. He shall require a report to be made to him at the hour of locking up the prisoners for the night, that they and all officers for duty are present, and that everything is correct in the prison and prison grounds. He shall direct that the prison be locked for the night, and the keys placed in secure keeping at 10 o'clock every night. He shall not allow ingress or egress between the hours of locking at night and unlocking in the morning, except to superior authorities, or to the medical officer, when on duty; and in special cases; the latter to be entered in his journal. *(To inspect the prison daily, and require reports to be given in. Hours of locking and unlocking the prison.)*

9. He shall visit the hospital daily, and see that proper arrangements are made for the safe custody of the sick prisoners, and that discipline is maintained, so far as is consistent with the medical treatment prescribed for them. He shall on all occasions support and assist the medical officer in the performance of his duties, and shall consult him respecting the quality of the provisions furnished to the prisoners. He will also from time to time with the steward, see that the issues of medical comforts are in order accordance with the orders of the medical officer, and that there has been no excess in any such issues, especially in such articles as wine, spirits, &c. *(To visit the hospital.)*

10. He shall frequently visit the prisoners while at labour, and make himself acquainted with the nature of the work to be performed by them, communicating with the warders under whom the prisoners are employed. *(To visit the prisoners while at work.)*

11. He shall enforce a high degree of cleanliness in every part of the prison, and also, with respect to the persons of the prisoners, their clothing, bedding, and everything else in use. *(Cleanliness.)*

12. He shall take every precaution necessary for preventing escape: and shall cause a daily examination to be made of the cells, windows, bars, bolts, locks, &c.; and he shall require each day at lock-up certificates from all warders in charge of works that such examination has been carefully made by them. He shall see that no ladders, planks, wheelbarrows, ropes, chains, implements or materials of any kind likely to facilitate escape are left unnecessarily exposed at any time in the yards or elsewhere. All such articles, when not in use, must be kept in their appointed places. He shall also adopt proper precautions against fire, and take care that the fire-engine and fittings are kept in an effective state, and that the proper officers and the prisoners are periodically exercised in working them. He shall take care that a proper supply of water is at all times maintained, *(Security of the prisoners, and precautions against fire.)*

talned, also that the crank pump is at all times in working order, and that any defect in the steam-engine is at once remedied.

Not to allow visitors to officers deep within the prison.

13. He shall not permit any person to remain for the night in the apartments of any officer within the prison, without written permission from superior authority; such permission to be entered in his journal. Nor shall any subordinate officer or servant occupying any Government quarters attached to the prison be allowed to keep a shop or a school, or to have any person, not a regular member of his family, sleeping in his quarters without special leave; or on any account to be lodging therein.

Intercourse with prisoners.

14. Excepting under special circumstances, and as permitted by the prison rules, he shall not allow any person, except the judges of the Court of Queen's Bench, the Common Pleas, and the Exchequer, and the Bishop of the Diocese, to enter the prison, or converse with a prisoner, without a written order from the Secretary of State, the director, or the Inspector. He shall have power to remove from the prison any visiter to the prison or to a prisoner, whose conduct is improper, noting the same in his journal.

May suspend subordinate officers.

15. He shall, in case of misconduct, have power to suspend any subordinate officer, but shall report the particulars without delay through the inspector to the director; and every officer or servant so suspended shall immediately give up his keys.

May punish prisoners for prison offences.

16. He shall have power to punish a prisoner for offences against the prison rules, and may order any prisoner so offending to be punished, by being closely or otherwise confined in a dark or light cell, or by being fed on bread and water only, or by such punishments, for any term not exceeding three days, and by forfeiture of marks, as hereafter directed; but a prisoner is not to be employed at severe hard labour while on bread and water. In a case of absolute necessity he may put a prisoner in irons, not to be continued on an offender for a longer period than 24 hours, without the written order of a director, specifying the cause thereof and the time during which the prisoner is to be kept in irons, which order shall be preserved by the governor as his warrant. He shall have authority to place any prisoner in separate confinement in the cells provided for the purpose, for a period not exceeding seven days; recording each case in which he may consider it necessary to exercise discretionary power in his journal. If a longer period of separation should be deemed by him to be desirable, he will apply to a director, who will give such directions thereupon as he may deem expedient.

Whenever he shall confine any offender, or shall punish him by changing his diet for more than 24 hours, he shall give notice thereof in writing to the medical officer, in order that he may see such prisoner as hereinafter directed.

To attend corporal punishment.

17. He shall attend all corporal punishment inflicted within the prison; and he shall enter in his journal the hour at which the punishment is inflicted, the number of lashes, and any orders which the medical officer may have given on the occasion.

Introduction of spirits and other forbidden articles.

18. He shall see that a warder-bound is kept affixed in some conspicuous place, near the entrance gate, cautioning persons from bringing spirits, fermented liquors, tobacco, letters, or other prohibited articles, into the prison. He may apprehend any person so offending, or who may attempt, by any means, to introduce into the prison letters, or other prohibited articles, and he shall take the person so apprehended before a justice of the peace. He shall not give permission for the introduction of prohibited articles, except (under approved regulations) for the use of the officers or servants, or on the requisition of the medical officer for the use of the sick.

To read letters.

19. He (or some other officer of the prison duly authorized by a director) shall read every letter addressed to or written by a prisoner, erasing the former, when read, in the chaplain of the religious persuasion to which the prisoner may belong, and receiving from him the letter, marking all such letters with his initials. He shall use his discretion in communicating to a prisoner, at any time, the contents of any letter addressed to such prisoner, but all cases in which he may think it proper to withhold a letter, which according to the rules may be received or written by a prisoner, shall be noted by him in his journal. He shall also enter in his journal any instance in which he may think fit to refuse admission to the friends of a prisoner, and the cause thereof, if the regulated time has elapsed since such prisoner had received a visit to the prison. Money that may be remitted to the governor or chaplain, for the use of a prisoner, shall be placed to the prisoner's credit, and accounted for on his discharge.

Illness of officers or prisoners. List of prisoners to be furnished to chaplain and medical officer.

20. He shall cause to be notified to the medical officer, without delay, the sudden illness of any officer or prisoner; and shall furnish to him a daily list of the prisoners reported sick in the prison. He shall also furnish to the chaplain and medical officer, on their visits to the prison, lists of such prisoners as are placed under punishment; all such lists to be signed by him or by the chief warder.

To notify particular cases to the medical officer.

21. He shall call the attention of the medical officer to the case of any prisoner whose state of health in mind or body appears to require his attention; and he shall note in his journal all such cases, with the results of examination by the medical officer.

32. He

* Under new rules (1862), the governor is empowered to keep a prisoner in separate confinement for 28 days.

22. He shall carry into effect the written directions of the medical officer for separating prisoners labouring under infectious, contagious, or mental diseases, or suspected thereof; and shall immediately give directions for cleaning, disinfecting, and limewashing any places occupied by such prisoners; and for washing, disinfecting, fumigating, or destroying any bed or suspected apparel or bedding. *To carry into effect the directions of the medical officer as to cleaning, &c.*

23. He shall carry into effect the written requisitions of the medical officer as to the supply of any additional bedding, or clothing, or alteration of diet for any prisoner, or with the approval of the director with respect to any alteration of discipline or treatment in the case of any prisoner whose mind or body appears to require it, or to be injuriously affected by the discipline; and he shall immediately report in writing to a director the case of any prisoner thus affected.

24. Upon the death of any prisoner within the prison, he shall give immediate notice thereof to the director, to the coroner of the district, and, when practicable, to the nearest relatives of the deceased. He shall see that an officer of the prison, or any prisoner, is a juror on any inquest which may be held on the body of any prisoner who shall have died in the prison. He shall take the necessary measures, in concurrence with the chaplain of the religious persuasion to which the prisoner belonged, for the decent interment of the body, in such burial ground as may be appointed for the purpose. *To give notice of the death of a prisoner.*

25. He shall keep a "Prisoners' Property Book," for the entry of all money and articles belonging to prisoners on their admission, or afterwards sent for their use; and the book shall show how all such property may have been disposed of. *Property book.*

26. He shall keep a "Journal" for recording all matters of importance within the prison, particularly such as relate to the health, discipline, or employment of the prisoners; their removal from one class to another; the prisoners who may be placed in separate confinement; the infringement, from whatever cause, of any of the prison rules; and also all punishments inflicted by him or other authority, referring for particulars of such cases to the Prisoners' Misconduct Report Book. *Journal.*

27. He shall keep a "Character Book," in the prescribed form, and enter therein concisely his observations on the character and conduct of every prisoner, for the purpose of preserving such a record of the particulars as shall guide him in a proper classification of the prisoners during their confinement, and in conferring good-conduct badges on those who deserve them. *Character book.*

He shall take every opportunity of impressing on the prisoners that the particulars of their conduct are thus entered and recorded, and that whilst no effort to obtain marks by good conduct and industry on the part of a prisoner will be disregarded by the authorities of the prison, every act of wilful misconduct and punishment will be equally noted.

The importance of the character book is obvious; and is meant in the governor's own, in making this record, closely to consider every circumstance of the man, and to prevent the operation of favour and caprice in the reports on which he must partly form his judgment of the merits of each individual.

28. He shall enter in a book, to be called the "Governor's Order Book," all his orders relative to the management and discipline of the prison; and from this book the entries shall be copied daily by the proper officers, who shall sign the same in acknowledgment of their having received the orders for the information of the other officers and servants of the several departments. *Governor's order book.*

29. He shall keep a "Prison Officers' Misconduct Book," and may fine subordinate officers and servants in any amount not exceeding 5s., for neglect of duty, or other offence against the prison rules; the amount of the fine to be applied as may from time to time be directed. *Subordinate officers' misconduct book.*

He shall report quarterly through the inspector to a director, on the conduct, character, and qualifications of the discipline officers, noting whether they perform their duties with such zeal and intelligence as will entitle them to future promotion in the convict service. This report will be accompanied by an abstract of the offences entered in the Officers' Misconduct Book, showing the fines or other punishments inflicted. He will, also, notice their state of health and ability to perform their duty, and call upon the medical officer to examine such as appear unequal to it; the abstract will also show the number of days each officer has been absent from duty, distinguishing absences on leave from those caused by illness. *Report quarterly on the conduct, &c., of the officers.*

30. He shall report through the inspector to the directors every month on the abilities, qualifications, and character of all the discipline officers who shall be serving on probation in the prison, specifying whether they are likely to become really good and efficient officers or otherwise; or whether in consequence of their general character, habits, temper, or disposition, it may be desirable that their services should be dispensed with, even previous to the expiration of the period appointed for their probation. *Report monthly on the abilities and qualifications of officers serving on probation.*

31. He shall keep a "Prisoners' Misconduct Book," for the entry of all offences committed by prisoners, and the manner in which such cases may have been disposed of. *Prisoners' misconduct book.*

In every case where a prisoner has been reported for admonition or placed in cells pending the governor's inquiry, full particulars will be given in the "Misconduct Book,"

329.　　　　G

even though the prisoner should be held not to be guilty of the offence, and the result of the inquiry must be stated.

Register and description books. Returns.

32. He shall keep a "Prison Register," and a "Description Book of Prisoners," in the prescribed forms, and all other books that may be required by a director; and shall send in to the proper authorities all such returns or reports as they may from time to time require from him.

Account books.

33. He shall keep such account books for the entry of all payments and receipts as may be required of him by the authorities; and shall render such accounts (accompanied by proper vouchers) as they may consider necessary. He may at any time call for and examine the accounts kept in any department of the establishment.

To examine the steward's books, and to debit himself with money received for prisoners. To keep letters written and received.

34. He will be required to examine all bills and accounts previously to their being paid. He will make a quarterly examination of the steward's books, and affix his signature thereto; he will also ascertain by weekly inspection that the steward's books are duly posted. He will also debit himself with all money received on behalf of prisoners.

35. He shall duly keep all official letters addressed to him, and cause to be entered in the letter book copies of all official letters that may be written by him, or under his direction.

To be responsible for the safe custody of journals and other documents.

36. He shall be responsible for the safe custody of the registers, journals, account books, and all other books and documents required to be kept by him, or confided to his care; and see that they are preserved unmutilated and unaltered; and shall, when required by superior authority, produce such books and documents for inspection. He shall see that a catalogue is kept of all books and printed papers allowed to the prisoners.

To have assistants in his office.

37. He shall have such assistants as may be deemed necessary for carrying on the general business of his office.

Inventories and accounts of stores.

38. He shall see that the steward takes inventories of all articles of stores, furniture, &c., under his charge, and he shall examine and sign the same, and transmit them to the directors, with any remarks that he may think proper to add thereto, as soon as possible after the 31st of March in each year. He shall also see that the steward keeps and renders the required accounts of all stores, and that he brings forward for periodical inspection such as are unserviceable or repairable, in order that they may be condemned or ordered to be repaired; also that the condemned stores are disposed of as may be directed; and he shall immediately bring to the notice of a director any deficiency that may come to his knowledge; he shall also at certain periods take stock of the stores' articles in use, and ascertain carefully that a proper account has been kept of the receipts and issue of such articles. He shall require from the steward monthly a certificate that he has examined and entered all tools and implements, all furniture, &c., in charge of the various warders, stating whether they are in good order, and detailing any deficiencies.

Survey of provisions, &c.

39. He shall inspect the provisions furnished for the prisoners; and in case any complaints shall be made to him respecting the quantity or quality of any article delivered for the use of the prison, he shall convey the same, with the aid of the medical officer and such person or persons as he may think fit to call on for the purpose of assisting his judgment, and shall give such directions as may appear to him upon such survey to be necessary, entering the complaint and the proceedings thereupon in his journal.

So far as possible, the governor, or officer in charge of the prison, shall invariably inspect the bread, meat, and milk, before these articles are received into store from the contractor; this is not in any way to relieve the steward from the responsibility of seeing that articles strictly according to contract only are received.

To promote economy in the prison.

40. He shall promote the utmost economy in every department, and carefully examine all demands submitted for his approval; he shall report to a director, without delay, any instances of waste or of carelessness of any public property by any prison officer which he may detect.

In case of emergency to apply to directors or inspector.

41. He shall freely communicate with the directors and inspector in all matters relating to the prison, apprising them of any matter of importance; and in case of any emergency not sufficiently provided for in the rules, he shall apply to them, and conform to their orders; acting, if necessary, in the meantime, to the best of his own judgment, according to the circumstances of the case.

42. The governor, or officer in charge of the prison in his absence, shall invariably attend at the first parade of warders in the morning, and other parades should occasionally be attended. Particular attention should be taken that all warders appear neatly and properly dressed, and that their uniforms are in proper order.

43. The governor shall frequently examine the warders' books (hereafter described); he shall, when going round the prison, from time to time, call upon the warders to produce their books, and he shall take especial care that entries once made are not erased or altered.

44. He

44. He will be held responsible that no trees or shrubs are trained or grown on any part of the interior or exterior prison walls, and that no rubbish is placed against them.

*45. He shall submit to the directors, on or before the 10th of January in each year, a report in writing, specifying, with reference to the preceding year, the conduct of the subordinate officers; the number of prisoners admitted to his custody, and their disposal; the manner in which their recaptive sentences have been carried into execution; the treatment of the prisoners; the species of labour on which they have been employed; the amount and particulars of their earnings; the state and condition of the buildings, &c.; the repairs or alterations which have been made, or may be required; the expenses of the prison; any abuse or abuses which he may have observed, or of which he may have received intimation in the management of the same; the number of escapes or attempts at escape; as well as the general state of the prisoners, as to morals, discipline, employment, proficiency in trades, and observance of the rules; together with a certificate, signed by himself, containing a declaration that the rules laid down for the government of the prison have been complied with in every instance, except in such cases as have been distinctly reported to, or brought under the notice of a director.

THE CHAPLAINS.

1. Each chaplain shall be a clergyman approved by lawful authority; he shall not, without the permission of the director, hold any other preferment with cure of souls, nor will he be permitted to take pupils. He shall reside at the prison if the director shall so direct. — *To hold no other preferment, &c.*

2. He shall be subject to no control in matters strictly within his department but that of the Chief Secretary or of the director. He shall represent to the director, and to the inspector and governor, whatever may appear to him to be worthy of their notice, or suggest anything which he may conceive likely to prove beneficial to the prisoners, or tend to their reformation or industrial training; but he shall take care not to interfere with the established rules and regulations of the prison as to security, or the routine of discipline and labour. He shall also be careful to conform to all such rules himself, as far as they apply to him. — *Control to which he is subject.*

3. He shall perform Divine service according to the rites of his church, and preach a sermon or give religious instruction in the chapel, or other appointed place, both morning and evening (unless specially attempted by the director) every Sunday in the year, and every holiday of his church, at such hours as shall be appointed. Prayers shall also be read by the chaplain, or in his absence, by the senior principal warder, or warder of the same religious persuasion, at the appointed times. He, or in his absence, the infirmary warder, or the senior principal warder, or warder of the same religious persuasion, shall also read prayers daily in the infirmary. — *To perform Divine service in the chapel. Read morning and evening prayers.*

The governor shall be responsible that arrangements are made, in conjunction with the chaplain, that the reading of prayers, and the religious attendance on the sick in the infirmary, are conducted so that prisoners of different religious persuasions shall not be annoyed thereby.

4. The chaplain shall keep an accurate register of the burials of all prisoners belonging to their respective churches who may die in the prison, and they shall, if required, attend at the interment of such prisoners. — *Burials.*

5. He shall endeavour, by all means in his power, and particularly by communing with their confidence, to obtain an intimate knowledge of the character and disposition of each prisoner under his care, and he is expected to allot a considerable portion of his time to visiting, admonishing, and instructing such prisoners. Whenever he shall be desirous of assembling any number of prisoners for the purposes of admonition and religious instruction, he shall notify, in writing, his wish upon that subject to the governor, who shall thereupon give the necessary orders for their being so assembled, taking care not to interfere with the hours appointed for labour, exercise, or rest. In case there shall be a difference of opinion between the chaplain and a director with respect to the religious books or papers proper to be admitted for the use of prisoners belonging to his church, reference shall be had to his bishop, or other ecclesiastical authority. — *To visit prisoners and direct the means of religious instruction to be given.*

6. He shall be at liberty to visit the schools daily, and inspect the course of instruction to be pursued in them, but shall not interfere with it. Should he, however, find any cause for complaint, he shall make it known to a director. — *Visits to schools.*

7. He shall keep a "journal" of all occurrences of importance within his observation or knowledge, and shall enter therein, from time to time, such particulars or observations as to the character, conduct, and progressive improvement of the prisoners during their confinement — *To keep a journal.*

* Amended 1862. See form Table at page 76.

confinement as he may think desirable. He shall also insert the date of the death of such as may die within the prison, with entries of the interment of each. His journal, and other documents that may be required, shall be submitted to the director or inspector, and he shall make such periodical or other reports as from time to time may be required of him.

To visit prisoners under punishment.
8. He shall visit daily any prisoner of his church who may be separated under punishment or special discipline, or to mend amount for any offence committed in the prison.

The chaplain to be informed on moral state of the prisoner.
9. It being of the utmost importance that the chaplain should be fully informed concerning the moral state of the prisoners, the governor shall communicate to him, without delay, all such occurrences as may appear to render his interposition expedient. The subordinate officers are also required to give the chaplain the earliest information on such subjects, when they shall meet him in the parts of the prison to which they respectively belong.

Absence, how to be supplied.
10. In case of absence from the prison on leave, he shall, if required, name a substitute, to be approved by the director or inspector, and in the event of being accidentally prevented from performing his duty, by illness or otherwise, he shall notify the same to the governor and record the cause of the absence in his journal, and on such occasions he should provide some other clergyman to perform his duty, and report in writing his name to the governor. He may with the sanction of a director, except the occasional assistance of a clergyman in the discharge of any part of his duties in the chapel, inserting the name of such clergyman in his journal.

To administer the sacrament.
11. The chaplain of the Established Church shall administer the sacrament of the Lord's Supper in the chapel, once in every quarter or oftener, at his discretion. The Roman Catholic chaplain shall administer the sacraments of his church subject to the direction of his bishop.

To communicate freely and confidentially with a director.
12. He shall freely and confidentially communicate with a director on all matters within his department, apprising him of any occurrence of importance affecting the moral or religious welfare of the prisoners.

The chaplain to make a yearly report.
†13. He shall submit to the directors, on or before the 10th day of January in each year, a report in writing, specifying, with reference to the preceding year, the religious and moral condition of the prisoners belonging to his church and the apparent effects of the discipline of the prison.

THE MEDICAL OFFICER.

General duties.
1. He shall be the resident medical officer of the Mountjoy Male and Female Convict Prisons; he shall not hold any other office or take private practice. He shall reside at the prisons, and attend all sick prisoners, and all officers and servants of the prisons, and their families resident at or within half a mile of the establishment. He shall have the general care of the health of the prisoners; and shall report to a director, and make known to the governor or superintendent any circumstances connected with the prison, or the treatment of the prisoners which shall at any time appear to him to require consideration on medical grounds.

To certify the state of health of prisoners newly received.
2. Every prisoner, sent sent from a convict prison, shall on admission be kept separate, until examined by the medical officer, and certified by him as fit to be received among the other prisoners. Others shall be examined as soon as possible after their arrival.

To examine prisoners recently admitted, and to keep a medical character book.
3. He shall make arrangements with the governor and superintendent for carefully inspecting all prisoners immediately on admission into the prison, and shall examine into their state of health, and shall enter an account of the same in the "Medical Character Book." He shall also insert therein such information respecting their health previous to admission, and their liability to be affected by any constitutional, bodily, or mental disorder, as may be received with the prisoners, or as he may be able to obtain from the prisoners themselves.

Prisoners received unfit, to be reported.
4. In the event of a prisoner being found on admission to have been in an unfit state to be sent to the prison, or to be mentally ill or otherwise than as described in the papers received with him, the medical officer will immediately report the case in writing to the governor or superintendent and take such measures as he may deem advisable, until further instructions can be received.

Periods of attendance.
5. He shall see the "complaining sick" every morning before nine o'clock, reporting to the governor or superintendent in writing as to their treatment. He shall visit the sick in the infirmary at such times as may be necessary and convenient; and he shall attend at all times, on receiving information of the serious illness of any prisoner or officer.

officer. He shall also be in attendance when required, to meet the superior authorities of the prison.

6. Orders for removal of prisoners to and from the infirmary shall be on printed forms stitched in a book, from which the part of the leaf containing the order shall be cut off, and a corresponding entry made on the duplicate part of the leaf; and every such order shall be signed by the medical officer, and given to the proper officer of the division or part of the prison to which the prisoner belongs. Removals from the infirmary shall take place at such hour as may be determined to be convenient. *Orders for the removal of prisoners to and from the infirmary.*

7. The medical officer shall insert in his own handwriting, in the prescription book, all orders for administering medicines to the prisoners; and he shall compound all medicines required by those whom he is bound to attend under rule No. 1. *To insert prescriptions in a book, &c.*

8. He shall give all necessary directions, in writing, respecting the diet, clothing, work, and exercise of any sick prisoner not removed to the infirmary, which directions he shall cause to be laid before the governor or superintendent, who shall thereupon act upon the same, unless they shall seem objectionable in point of discipline. In such case the governor or superintendent shall forthwith confer with the medical officer, and if necessary, refer the question to a director; and in the meantime the prisoner shall be removed to the infirmary. *Directions respecting the diet, &c. of sick prisoners not removed to the infirmary.*

9. At the end of each week he shall cause to be delivered to the governor or superintendent a list of all extra articles, such as wine, beer, fish, fruit, &c., issued to sick prisoners, with the names of such patients, and the quantities consumed by each during the week. *Consumption of extra articles.*

10. Whenever the medical officer shall have reason to believe that either the mind or the body of a prisoner is likely to be injuriously affected by the discipline or treatment observed in the prison, he shall report the case, in writing, to the governor or superintendent accompanied by such suggestions as he may think the case require. The governor or superintendent shall thereupon alter or suspend the discipline, and regulate the work, as regards such prisoner accordingly, and report the same as directed. *Removal of prisoners from under the ordinary discipline on account of mental or bodily infirmity.*

11. He shall give directions, in writing, for immediately separating from the other prisoners any prisoner having, or suspected of having, infectious, contagious, or mental diseases; and for cleansing, disinfection, and white-washing any places occupied by such prisoners, as well as for cleansing, disinfecting, or destroying any infected bedding or clothing. *To give directions in cases of infectious diseases.*

12. He shall keep a "medical register" in which he shall enter, or cause to be entered, the names of all prisoners in the infirmary, and of all those who are receiving medicines, or other articles appropriated to the use of the sick in the wards or cells; and he shall also enter, or cause to be entered, in such register, in the English language day by day, an account of the state of every sick prisoner, the name of his disease, and a description of the medicines, diet, and any other treatment which he may order for each prisoner; also the date of every removal to the infirmary, and of every discharge therefrom. He shall sum up daily in such register the number of prisoners in the infirmary, and the number under medical treatment in other parts of the prison. *Register.*

He shall keep a "journal," in which he shall enter all matters of importance in regard to the health of the prisoners; and also make out and transmit, through the governor or superintendent to a director, a monthly summary of the numbers of sick admitted to the infirmary, or treated in the other parts of the prison. His register and journal shall be submitted to a director when required. *Journal.*

13. He shall furnish to the governor and superintendent daily a morning report, on the prescribed form, of sick prisoners admitted, discharged, and remaining in the infirmary, and the other parts of the prison. *Morning report of the sick.*

14. He shall, on Monday in every week, or as soon after as may be convenient, inspect every part of the prison, for the purpose of ascertaining that nothing exists therein likely to be injurious to the health of the prisoners, and especially that the ventilation is sufficiently provided for and properly attended to. The result of this inspection shall be recorded in his journal. He shall see every prisoner on such occasions, and shall thereupon report, in writing, to a director, or other superior authority, the general state of health of the prisoners, and any circumstances connected with the state of the prison, which shall appear to him to require consideration on medical grounds. He shall also frequently visit the kitchen at such times as may be convenient, for the inspection of provisions, cooked and uncooked, reporting thereupon to the governor or superintendent when necessary. *General weekly inspection.*

15. He shall make a weekly inspection of all the prisoners, so as to ascertain their general state of health, that they are clean in their persons, and free from disease. *Weekly inspection.*

16. On receiving notice of any prisoner being under confinement for any prison offence, or in separate confinement, he shall visit such prisoner daily while such punishment shall be continued. *To visit prisoners under punishment.*

To attend corporal punishment.

17. He shall attend all corporal punishments within the prison; and his instructions for preventing injury to health shall be obeyed.

To report the illness of subordinate officers to the governor or superintendent.

18. When he shall observe, or be called on to attend any subordinate officer or servant of the establishment who may be incapacitated by illness for the performance of his duties, he shall report upon the nature of such illness to the governor or superintendent, and shall afterwards report from time to time on the state of such officer's or servant's health and ability to return to duty.

To report on particular cases.

19. If any prisoner shall be afflicted with any disorder from which he is not likely to be sufficiently recovered to quit the infirmary, or go to work, during the usual term of confinement in the prison, the medical officer shall make, through the governor or superintendent, a special report of the circumstances of the case to a director, with a view to the prisoner being removed to an invalid establishment, or otherwise disposed of, as may appear desirable.

To notify cases of danger to the chaplain.

20. He shall give notice to the chaplain to whom faith the prisoner may belong when any case of sickness appears to him to warrant an import of danger.

Additional medical aid.

21. If any case of peculiar difficulty or danger should occur, he shall have power to call in additional aid, referring previously to a director for approbation, and for sanction as to the amount of the fee, in every case which will reasonably admit of such reference. No operation endangering life shall be performed without a previous consultation with another medical practitioner, except under very urgent circumstances, not admitting of delay; such circumstances to be recorded in his journal.*

To report on the death of any prisoner.

22. He shall, after the death of any prisoner, enter in his journal a written report, containing the following particulars, viz. :—As what time the deceased was taken ill; when the circumstance was first communicated to him; where the complaints assumed a dangerous aspect; whether there were any special circumstances connected with his disease which required observation; what opinion he formed of the case; when the prisoner died; when the coroner sat, the verdict given, and what observations (if any) were made by the coroner, or the jury, upon the subject.

Examination of prisoners previous to removal.

23. When prisoners are removed from the prison, he shall duly examine them, and certify as to their fitness to leave the prison, and as to such other particulars regarding them as may be required.

Receipts and expenditure of medicines.

24. He shall keep regular accounts of the receipt and expenditure of all medicines and other medical stores; and shall be responsible that sufficient requisitions are made by him (through the governor or superintendent) in due time to ensure there being always a proper supply of medical stores in the prison. He shall from time to time examine the medicines kept in the surgery, in order to assure himself of their purity.

Orders for diet and other articles.

25. Orders for diet, and all other articles required in the medical department, shall be signed by him.

Absence.

26. If prevented from attending to his duties, by illness or other unavoidable cause, he shall communicate the circumstance without delay to the governor and superintendent, and shall submit, through the governor to a director, the name and address of a substitute, for approval.

To report any irregularity in the infirmary.

Arrangement of general duties.

27. He shall report to the governor or superintendent any irregularity in the infirmary which may come to his knowledge, of any difficulty or obstruction which he may meet with in the performance of his duty; and he shall consult with the governor or superintendent, and arrange his general visits and duties so as not to disturb the routine of discipline, or interfere with the regular hours of labour.

To examine subordinate officers before commencing their duties, and candidates for situations in which of the prison.

28. He is to examine all subordinate officers appointed to the establishment, before they commence their duties; and, when required, all candidates for employment as subordinate officers or servants of the prison, who may be sent to him for that purpose, and report whether they possess the necessary qualifications as to health and strength, and shall make an annual report, on or before the 10th January, on the state of health of all the subordinate officers and servants, and their capability to perform their duties.

Temporary absence.

29. Whenever he shall temporarily absent himself from the prison, he shall leave notice at the surgery with the infirmary warder and with the hospital matron where he may be found in the event of his services being required.

Annual report.

30. He shall submit to the directors, on or before the 10th January in each year, a report in writing, specifying, with reference to the past year, the state of health in which the prisoners have been received, and the general state of health that has been maintained; the disorders which have been most prevalent; whether any contagion can be traced

* Approved in present form, 1872.
† Amended 1865. *See new rule at page 79.*

traced between the diseases which have occurred and the locality or actual state of the buildings, or the diet, employment, or other particular circumstances; the number of deaths; the number of infirmary cases; the number of cases of slight indisposition treated in the wards; and the proportion of sick in the whole number of prisoners during the year; or any other circumstances with reference to the health of the prisoners that he may consider proper to bring under the attention of the authorities.

THE STEWARD.

1. He shall give such security for the due performance of the duties of his office as shall be required. He shall be resident at the prison, and shall not be concerned, either directly or indirectly, in any business, occupation, or employment whatsoever, other than such as belongs to his office. He shall receive, examine, and take particular account of all stores connected with the victualling, clothing, &c., of the prisoners, as well as of all rations and supplies of every description to be issued to the several officers and servants, and shall be responsible for all deficiencies. He shall immediately report to the governor any defect in quality, or deficiency in the weight or measure of any articles, or irregularity in the delivery, and take his directions thereupon. He shall issue at the times appointed, on demands signed or countersigned by the governor, or, in his absence, the chief warder, the proper supplies; and he shall take care that no articles of clothing or other goods are issued from his stores, until they have been properly marked with the prison marks.

The steward to give security, and to have his receipt checked, and delivery of stores.

2. He shall not, directly or indirectly, have any interest in any contract or agreement for the supply of the prison; nor shall he receive, directly or indirectly, under any pretence whatsoever, any fee or gratuity or present from any contractor, or person tendering any contract with the establishment, nor from any prisoner or prisoner's friend, nor from any person visiting the prison.

Shall not have any interest in contracts, nor receive fees or gratuities from tradesmen, &c.

3. The steward shall keep all books of account, or of stores, which he may be required to keep by the governor or a director, and all demands made upon him shall be on prescribed forms, which shall be kept as vouchers. He shall send in demands monthly to the governor, for all articles and stores wanted in his departments, particularizing, when required on all such demands, the quantities (if any) of the articles demanded then remaining in store, and stating whether serviceable or unserviceable; and shall furnish all returns as may be directed from time to time.

To keep books of accounts, and make demands for all articles wanted.

4. He shall also enter in his accounts, and deliver to the chaplain or principal school-master, any books ordered for the use of the prisoners; and shall receive, enter, and deliver to the proper officer any medicines ordered by the medical officer. He shall take care that all empty bottles, phials, pots, jars, and boxes are duly returned to the proper parties, and that the usual allowances are made in the bills for the articles so returned.

Supply of books and medicines.

5. The bread and other provisions for the prisoners shall be delivered to the cook, accompanied by notes stating the quantities. He shall receive from the chief warder or the principal warder, daily, a return of the rations to be provided for the following day.

Delivery of provisions to cook.

6. He shall give in, weekly, an account of the provisions consumed in the preceding week, with a statement of the number of prisoners on full or reduced diet, and the number and description of officers and servants dieted; also an account of all articles issued for the use of the infirmary during the preceding week, or to the officers of the prison. All his account books, receipts and issues of provisions, materials, and Government stores, shall be brought weekly to the governor's office for examination at such time as may be appointed; and if in arrear, he shall at once time make a written report, detailing any omissions and explaining the cause thereof.

Weekly account of provisions to be given in.

7. All articles belonging to the prison, which are from time to time sent to the wash, shall be delivered by the steward or appointed officer to the person or persons employed to wash the same, and shall, when washed, be delivered back to him for issue to the different parts of the prison. He shall take care to keep a duplicate of every washing bill delivered to him; and whenever any article shall not be returned from the wash, he shall make immediate inquiry respecting the same, and report to the governor if the reply be not satisfactory.

To send and receive back all articles to and from the wash.

8. He shall keep a correct inventory of all clothing, furniture, tools, and utensils in the prison, which shall show the several parties responsible for the same, and be signed by them. No article whatever shall be taken out of such inventory, without the written directions of the governor, until condemned by proper authority, and finally disposed of or destroyed after such condemnation. The condemnation to be made as soon as possible after the termination of each quarter, after which, a statement of the articles so condemned will be signed by the members of the Board of Survey (of whom the governor shall be one), and submitted for the director's information, when, if approved, the condemned articles shall be regularly written off the prison stock books. The steward shall make a survey, prepare inventories of all the stores, and of all the furniture, &c., there mentioned, and shall sign and deliver the same to the governor as soon as practicable after the 31st of March in each year. All officers shall be responsible for the stores in the

To keep a correct inventory of furniture.

Regulations for condemnation of stores, &c.

Inspection of quarters.

quarters allowed them or occupied by them, and shall be charged with any damage beyond reasonable wear that may be done to such quarters or the fixtures in them. An inspection and report on the quarters of the subordinate officers and servants shall be made every month by the steward, under the direction of the governor, and occasional inspections of particular quarters shall be made at such times as may be directed.

To promote economy in the steward.

8. As the saving of unusual expense in the wear and tear and consumption of articles used in the establishment depends chiefly on the vigilance, intelligence, and integrity of the steward, he shall consider it his duty to watch carefully the demands which are made on him, and to bring to the knowledge of the governor any circumstances which may demand notice, with a view to check unnecessary or improvident expenditure and to promote the utmost economy in every branch of the establishment.

Absence.

10. He shall not be absent from the prison during the prescribed hours for his attendance, unless permitted by the governor, or under such general regulations as to his absence as may from time to time be established.

Store-rooms.

11. He shall be responsible that the store-rooms, &c., in his department are kept in proper order, and all stores properly and systematically arranged therein.

To inspect scales, weights, and measures.

12. He shall from time to time inspect the various scales, weights, and measures in use throughout the prison, for the issue or distribution of provisions.

To perform the duties of a discipline officer.

13. He shall be liable to be called upon by the inspector or governor to perform the duties of a discipline officer, in cases of emergency.

14. In no case shall any article of clothing, tool, utensil, piece of furniture, or otherwise, be issued, unless the old article which it is intended to replace is first returned into store, excepting in the case of loss or destruction of any such articles, when a report will be at once made of such loss or destruction by the officer responsible, and the reports shall be filed in steward's office.

The steward shall keep a book showing the numbers of new articles issued, those returned to replace them, and date of report; the list shall also show the name of the officer reporting loss or destruction of articles not returned to store.

CLERKS AND ASSISTANT CLERKS.

1. They shall reside in or near the prison, shall be punctual and diligent in the performance of their duties, and shall attend in the prison at such hours as shall be appointed by the governor. In case of emergency they shall be liable to be called upon by the governor to do the duty of a discipline officer.

2. The senior clerk shall be held strictly responsible for the due and proper preparation of all accounts, returns, and other documents, in order that they may be furnished at the appointed dates. He shall also be responsible for the safe keeping of all documents committed to his charge, and shall see that the various office books are duly posted.

SCHOOLMASTER AND ASSISTANTS.

The school to be under the inspection of the National Board of Education.

1. The prison school shall be under the inspection of the National Board of Education; and an officer appointed by that department will occasionally examine and report on the conduct and management thereof, the progress of the prisoners, &c.

The general duties of the schoolmaster.

2. The principal schoolmaster and his assistants at Mountjoy Male Prison shall *reside* on or near the premises. Their time shall be employed under the direction of the inspector and governor, in the duties of their office, according to such regulations as may be prescribed by the directors.

To promote the improvement of prisoners.

3. They shall consider it a *chief part* of their duty to promote, as far as lies in their power, the moral improvement and instruction of the prisoners.

Books and stationery.

4. The principal schoolmaster shall, as may be ordered, take charge of the books and stationery that may be issued to him for the instruction and use of the prisoners, and issue such supplies of those articles to the prisoners, under the direction of the inspector and governor, as may be authorised. His accounts of the receipt of these articles, and of the manner in which they have been distributed, shall be regularly kept, and inspected from time to time by the inspector or governor, who shall affix to them his initials, and the date of his inspection. An annual account of the stock in hand shall be taken.

The principal schoolmaster to be answerable for the management of school.

5. The principal schoolmaster shall be responsible for the general conduct and management of the school.

6. The

6. The assistant schoolmasters shall obey all orders and instructions connected with their department, which they may receive from the principal schoolmaster.

7. The schoolmasters and assistants shall not leave the prison, without the permission of the governor, during the prescribed hours of their attendance.

8. The schoolmasters shall, in turn, if required, act as chapel clerks on Sundays and holidays.

9. In all matters affecting the discipline of the prison (whether in school or otherwise), they shall obey the orders of the governor, and they shall be careful to notice and report every infringement of the rules and regulations by the prisoners under their charge.

The assistants to obey the orders of the principal school-master.

Not to go out with-out leave during hours of attendance.

To maintain order.

THE CHIEF WARDER.

1. He shall constantly reside at the prison, and thoroughly acquaint himself with all the rules and Acts of Parliament relating to Convict Prisons.

2. He shall be the assistant to the governor on all occasions, and carry into effect his instructions, and shall see that his orders are strictly obeyed. He shall consider it a main part of his duty to exercise a sound moral influence over both the officers and the prisoners placed under his supervision. He shall frequently visit the prisoners in their cells, for the purpose of promoting, by his advice, the great object of their reformation. He shall restrain by his authority, every tendency to oppression or undue harshness on the part of officers, and likewise every tendency to levity, rudeness, and insubordination, on the part of the prisoners; and shall discourage, by his own example, and by the maintenance of a high moral standard, every disposition to deceit, falsehood, immorality, and idleness, constantly aiming to raise the minds of the prisoners to a sense of their responsibility, and of the comfort arising from a conscientious discharge of their duties.

He shall, so far as his other duties will permit him, constantly visit all parts of the prison at uncertain times; he shall, so far as he possibly can, prevent warders from speaking on prison matters, or on general subjects in the hearing of the prisoners.

3. He shall visit the workshops daily, and see that the prisoners are kept steadily to their labour. He shall diligently observe the behaviour of all the subordinate officers and servants, as well as of the prisoners. He shall see that they strictly adhere to the rules, and shall report immediately to the governor any neglect or misconduct that may come to his knowledge.

He shall also daily visit the hospital; also the garden and the portion of prisoners employed therein.

He shall occasionally inspect the outer walls (outside) of the prison, and shall cause a principal warder to do so daily, and to report to him whether the walls or gates appear to have been in any way tampered with from without.

To reside at the prison.

General duties.

To observe conduct of officers and prisoners, visit shops, grounds, &c.

4. He shall be responsible to the governor that the details of duties connected with order and discipline of the prison are carried on with promptness and regularity, and in strict accordance with the regulations of the establishment, and with a view to promote its object. He shall also enforce the utmost economy.

5. He shall see that all subordinate officers and warders immediately on joining the prison, and at all times afterwards, are fully instructed in their particular duties, and that they keep the required rolls, lists, and records of the work of the prisoners that they duly observe their character and industry, and make the required daily and other reports and returns in the proper manner and at the proper times.

He shall pay particular attention that the lock kept by each warder (as hereafter directed) is regularly filled daily by each officer; he shall frequently call on the warders to produce their books, and will each evening examine and countersign each book, returning the books at first parade daily.

To superintend details of duties.

Instruction of officers and warders in their duties

6. He shall prepare and furnish the necessary abstracts of these reports and returns, and make such daily periodical or special reports as may be required by the governor.

Reports and returns.

7. He shall see that the absence of the officers and entrance for their meals, or on other authorised occasions, takes place at the proper hours, and that they return to their duty at the appointed times, reporting any infringement of the rules in this respect.

To see that warders are present at proper hours.

8. He shall daily inspect every part of the prison, especially the cells and bedding, and that they are clean, and in order, and that the means of security in the different wards, yards, and workshops are effective.

Inspection of prison.

9. He shall see that the keys are securely disposed of for the night, under such regulations for this object as may be established by the governor, and it will be his duty to visit the prison by night whenever it is not visited by the governor.

Security of keys and nightly visits.

529.   U   10. He

10. He shall generally superintend the movements of the prisoners when passing to and from the workshops, and be careful that the movements are made with regularity and without loss of time.

Ration returns.

11. He shall receive and check, and cause to be delivered to the steward, daily, the returns of the rations required for the following day, and compare those of the preceding day with the actual total number of prisoners. He shall also notify to the steward any changes in the established number of rations for the officers and servants. He shall also check all demands made on the steward for stores or clothing to be used in the wards, and shall be held responsible that no extra clothing is issued to a prisoner without due authority of the governor or medical officer.

Meals, clothing, washing, shaving, and exercise of prisoners.

12. He shall also generally superintend the arrangements for the regular messing of the prisoners, and distribution of their meals. He shall take care that their clothing is in proper repair, their hair kept properly cut, their washing, shaving, and bathing attended to, according to the rules, and that the prescribed hours for their exercise are duly observed; and shall give his particular attention to all matters of detail connected with the interior economy of the prison; he shall frequently visit the prisoners when at exercise. He shall attend all parades, and shall see that all officers attend punctually and properly dressed.

Prisoners seeing their friends.

13. He shall give all necessary directions for permitting prisoners (agreeably to orders duly signed by the governor) to see their friends, taking care that all interviews take place in the presence of an officer. All improper communications are to be repressed, and the prisoner, if necessary, removed before the expiration of the prescribed time.

To report officers and prisoners' complaints, &c., to the governor.

14. He shall immediately report, for the governor's information and decision, any complaint made by officer or prisoner, and also the wish of any prisoner to speak to a director, inspector, or governor.

Prisoners' punishments, &c.

15. He shall specially attend to the carrying out all orders as to punishments to be inflicted on prisoners, and shall see that they have the exercise ordered in each case.

Absence.

16. On no occasion whatever shall he leave the prison during the temporary absence of the governor without the permission of the inspector, nor during the presence of the governor without his permission. When proceeding in the course of his duties outside the prison wall, he shall leave one of the principal warders to attend to the duties within the prison, with instructions where he is to be found in case of his presence being required.

Charge of prison in absence of governor.

17. If under any circumstances the governor and chief warder are both absent, the charge of the prison shall devolve on the senior principal warder, to whom it shall be regularly delivered over; but the exclusion of each delivery shall not justify such principal warder in neglecting the charge, if he should be aware that the governor and chief warder are actually absent from the prison.

To communicate with the governor.

18. He shall lose no time in communicating to the governor every circumstance which may come to his knowledge likely to affect the safety or health of the prisoners, the efficiency of the officers, or in any other way requiring the governor's attention; and he shall by his own example, and as far as he possibly can do so, check any tendency on the part of the warders to answer or question any order of their superiors.

To keep a journal.

19. He shall keep a journal, in which he shall enter briefly the occurrences of each day.

Counting prisoners, &c.

20. He shall require from the principal warders each evening at lock-up a return showing the number of prisoners in the prison; also from the senior hospital warder a return showing the number of prisoners under his charge in the hospital; from these documents he shall make a return, to hand to the governor, showing the total number of prisoners in custody at night; in the morning, in like manner, he will obtain returns showing the number of prisoners unlocked, and will hand to the governor a return showing the number of prisoners unlocked.

21. He shall at least once in every two months cause a strict search, under the immediate superintendence of himself and the principal warders, of every prisoner and occupied cell in the prison; also of all rooms in which prisoners are at any time. No prisoner or cell shall on these occasions be searched but in the presence of the chief or principal warden, nor shall any prisoner be allowed out of his cell until the entire body of prisoners and cells are searched. He shall on no account inform any officer of the day on which such search is to be made, the governor excepted. In event of any unauthorised article being found, or any prison property not duly issued, in a prisoner's possession, he shall at once report the same to the governor.

PRINCIPAL WARDERS AT MOUNTJOY MALE PRISON.

1. Each principal warder at Mountjoy Prison shall have allotted to him particular *General duties.* charge of each parts of the prison as the governor may direct, with a view to maintaining an effective supervision of the duties of the warders in charge of, or doing duty in, the wards or minor subdivisions of the prison, and of the conduct of the prisoners therein; and shall also perform such general duties in the establishment as may from time to time be directed. He shall keep rolls of the prisoners' names under his care, showing the ward, the trade, and the class to which each prisoner belongs. He shall see that the rules of the prison, and such orders as may be given to him by the inspector, governor, or chief warder from time to time are duly observed in his division; for the state of which, and for the regular performance of the duties of the officers attached thereto, as well as for their good conduct and demeanour, he shall be held responsible.

2. He shall keep an "Order Book," to be called the "Principal Warder's Order Book," *To keep a book for* into which he shall copy all such orders entered in the "Governor's General Order Book" *entering orders of* as relate to his division; and he shall be held responsible that the warders of his division *the governor.* are fully acquainted with all orders which have reference to their duties.

3. He shall keep a "Report Book," containing a detailed account of occurrences within *To report daily to* his division, founded upon the reports made to him by the warders, as hereinafter directed, *the governor.* and upon his own observations; which report book, together with a list of the sick belonging to his division, he shall carry to the chief warder, at such hour as may be appointed; and he shall also specially report during the day, through the chief warder, when practicable, any circumstance which may require the governor's or chief warder's immediate attention. He shall particularly notice in his daily report any injury done to the buildings or other parts of his division, or any article deficient or damaged therein; mentioning the name of any officer liable for such injury, deficiency, or damage, or of any prisoner who may have occasioned the same; and so long as repairs reported to be wanted shall remain undone, he shall continue to notice the same in his daily reports, unless directed by the governor or chief warder to discontinue to mention them. He shall also notice in his reports any inconvenience or difficulty arising, or likely to arise, from any of the rules, or from the orders he may have received.

4. He shall send in, through the chief warder, demands, on the approved form, to be *To demand articles* signed by the governor, addressed to the steward, for such articles of stores, &c., as may *wanted from the* be wanted in his division, limiting his requisitions to such as are necessary, and preventing *steward, and to* all waste or improvident expenditure. He shall return all articles worn out, when new *obtain renewal of* ones are demanded in their stead, or at such other times as may be directed. He shall *dangerous articles* make a special report, if his demands are not complied with in due course; and shall also *at lock-up.* report to the governor any irregularity in the receipt, or defect in the quality of the articles demanded.

He shall each evening at lock-up obtain a return in the prescribed form from each warder and trades warder in charge of prisoners in his division, showing the numbers of tools and any other articles under their charge; and shall be held responsible that all articles which may be considered to be unfit to remain in the prisoners' cells are placed in a secure place.

5. He shall receive with all articles from the steward a delivery note, with which he *To compare* shall compare the articles received; and shall regularly enter his receipts and issues in the *articles received* proper book, which book shall be produced at stated times, to be compared with the *with delivery note,* storekeeper's entries. *&c.*

6. He shall see that the prisoners of his division are duly supplied with all articles *To see that* allowed for their use; and he shall report immediately every instance in which any *prisoners are* prisoner shall be unemployed, with the cause thereof; and he shall also enter all such *employed.* cases in his report book.

7. He shall immediately report, for the governor's information, any complaint made by *To report prisoners'* a prisoner, and also the wish of any prisoner to speak to a director, inspector, or governor. *complaints to the* *governor.*

8. He shall check the number of prisoners in each party, when collected for their work, *To count and* and see that they are properly taken over in charge by the appointed warder. He shall *observe the parties.* visit the workshops frequently during the day.

He shall bear in mind that during the hours in which the prisoners are unlocked he should be as much as possible in the prison, visiting the wards, workshops, school, and grounds; a principal warder should invariably be on the grounds during general exercise hours, and he should visit the hospital at least once daily.

On the return of parties from the workshops he shall see that the numbers in each party are duly counted and checked.

He shall also, after lock-up in the evening, and after unlock in the morning, hand in a return showing the number of prisoners in his division.

58   COPY OF RULES AND REGULATIONS

To communicate to chief warder the illness of prisoners.

Removal of prisoners to and from infirmary.

10. He shall communicate without delay to the chief warder any instance that may come to his notice of a prisoner being out of health. He shall execute all orders which he may receive, signed by the medical officer, for the removal of prisoners to and from the hospital, delivering the order in the former case with the prisoner to the infirmary warder, and filing it in the latter case, after having been removed from the infirmary, in his warrant for the return of the prisoner to the division, and shall enter all such interval in his daily report book. In case of the sudden indisposition of any prisoner, he may remove such prisoner to the infirmary at his own discretion; but he shall give notice thereof as soon as possible to the chief warder or governor.

Treatment of sick officers not removed to infirmary.

11. He shall take care that all medicines, or medical applications, sent in for the use of prisoners whose illness is not so serious as to require their removal to the infirmary are delivered to the wardens of their respective wards (excepting in the cases where the medicines, &c., are administered by the hospital warder), and he shall see that all bottles, &c., in which such medicines are sent, are duly returned to the infirmary. In case the state of a prisoner's health shall appear to require any exemption from the ordinary rules of the prison, the necessary order to that effect will be given by the governor, on the representation of the medical officer.

To see that wardens are present at proper hours.

12. He shall see that the absence of the wardens and servants under his charge, for their meals or on other authorised occasions, takes place at the proper hours, and that they return to their duty at the appointed times, and report any infringement of the rules on the part of officers or prisoners without delay to the governor and chief warder.

Returns of rations and distribution of bread.

13. He shall prepare, at such hour daily as may be directed, proper returns of the number of rations to be provided for prisoners in his division on the following day, and deliver the same to the chief warder for delivery to the steward. He shall superintend the distribution of the prisoners' meals at their different meals; and see that any complaint made by a prisoner respecting his food is immediately reported to the governor and chief warder.

Attendance during visits to prisoners.

14. He shall, unless at such times as the chief warder performs such duty, be present during all visits permitted to prisoners by the written order of the governor, chief warder, or higher authority, and shall note in his report book the date of all such visits, and the names and numbers of the prisoners receiving visits.

To inspect frequently every part of the division, &c.

15. He shall frequently inspect every part of the division under his charge, and ascertain, by minute examination, that all locks, bars, bolts, and other means of security are in good order, that the furniture belonging thereto is complete, and that the prisoners have not in their possession any unauthorised articles, to which purpose he shall occasionally search the person of every prisoner. He shall constantly look into the stores, and all other places connected with the division, and see that they are in proper order; and shall also see that the wards are properly ventilated.

To attend to punishment of prisoners.

16. He shall pay particular attention to the due execution of the governor's orders with respect to the punishment of prisoners in his division, and give written instructions to the wardens, to ensure punishment being given with such orders; and he shall daily frequently visit all prisoners under punishment.

To communicate to chaplain the wish of any prisoner to speak with him, and report absence of prisoners from divine service.

17. He shall communicate to the governor, through the chief warder, any intimation he may receive from any prisoner wishing to speak with the chaplain of the religious persuasion to which he may belong on the next visit of the chaplain to the prison, and shall give in on all occasions a list of the prisoners of his division absent from divine service or prayers, noting therein the cause of such absence.

18. He shall see that all orders which he may receive respecting the employment and instruction of the prisoners are duly attended to.

19. He shall, by his own example and constant observation, check any familiar conversation between any officer and a prisoner, or any conversation between officers on prison affairs or general subjects in the hearing of prisoners; he shall also check at once any disposition on the part of officers to canvass or question any order given by their superiors.

Charge of prison in absence of the governor and chief warder.

20. If under any circumstances the governor and chief warder should be absent, the charge of the prison shall devolve on the principal warder appointed to do duty in such an emergency by the governor, to whom it shall be regularly delivered over; but the omission of such delivery shall not justify such principal warder in neglecting the charge, if he should be aware that they are actually absent from the prison.

THE WARDERS.

1. The warders shall have assigned to them the immediate charge (under the principal warders) of such prisoners, and of such parts of the prison, as the governor may direct, and shall be responsible for the maintenance of proper order and discipline. They shall each keep a book, in which they shall daily enter the name and number of each prisoner under their charge, stating his occupation each day; in these books they shall enter any event which they may have to make against a prisoner, or any unusual occurrence in their wards; in event of a prisoner being transferred either to or from their wards, they shall note to whom, or by whom, such prisoner was handed over; these books to be handed to the chief warder at least parade each evening; they shall also hand to the chief warder, at evening parade, a list showing all articles in their charge, whether for the personal use of the prisoners under their charge, or for their use as tradesmen, certifying that all dangerous articles, and all such as may by the governor or chief warder be ordered to be removed from the prisoners' cells, have been placed in security. They shall inspect, daily, the wards and other parts of the prison under their charge, together with the furniture and fittings therein, and shall minutely examine all the locks, bars, bolts, and other means of security. They shall state in their books that they have done so, and whether they found everything correct or otherwise. They shall be careful that the prisoners have not any prohibited articles in their possession, or secreted about the wards; and may, if necessary, search any prisoner. They shall report all instances of misconduct or breach of the rules, through the principal warders. They shall daily, in addition to the ordinary searches of prisoners, thoroughly search the person and drill of one or more prisoners, with the assistance of another warder, noting in their books the name and number of such prisoner, the date of search, and the warder by whom assisted; any inaccuracy in keeping up the above-mentioned books or returns will be invariably reported by the governor to a director, and dealt with by a director alone. They shall make also such returns relative to prisoners' labour, conduct, &c., as may be required from them.

2. The utensils and furniture provided for the use of the prisoners in each ward shall be considered as under the care of the warder of that particular ward; who shall state in his daily report to the principal warder any injury done thereto or to the buildings, or any articles deficient therein, mentioning the cause of such injury or deficiency, and by whom committed; and any such warder neglecting so to do shall be made accountable for the same.

3. They shall immediately communicate in writing to the principal warders the wish of any prisoner to speak with a director, the inspector, governor, or chaplain.

4. They shall give immediate notice to the chief and principal warders of any prisoner who may appear to them to be out of health; and in the absence of the principal warders, shall bring any case of sickness immediately to the notice of the medical officer; and in event of the absence of both these officers, to the hospital warder.

5. Warders shall not keep or use in the wards or workshops any article of food, or tobacco, or liquor of any kind; nor shall any newspaper, book, or other publication, be introduced by them into the wards, except the rules and regulations of the prison; any warder so doing shall be suspended.

6. They shall perform such further duties as may from time to time be prescribed by the director, inspector, or governor, for the purpose of preventing communication, encouraging industry, cleanliness, and order among the prisoners, and promoting the general objects of the establishment.

7. Warders

7. Warders shall be careful not to canvass or question any orders or regulations made by their superiors; they shall avoid speaking of prison matters outside the prison; also to avoid speaking of prison or general subjects before prisoners; and shall on no account whatever enter into familiar conversation with a prisoner.

Officers in charge of prisoners employed at trades.

8. The warders specially in charge of prisoners employed at trades, or otherwise, shall maintain due discipline, and require a proper amount of labour among such prisoners; and shall keep such books, lists, and accounts as may be directed, to show the conduct and industry of the prisoners, the amount of work done by them, and the expenditure of materials. When not actually engaged in these special duties, they shall perform all general prison duties in common with the other warders.

INFIRMARY WARDER.

To have charge of sick in the infirmary.

1. The infirmary warder shall have the charge of the sick in the infirmary, under the direction of the medical officer, and shall frequently visit any prisoner sick in the cells.

To have charge of drugs, stores, &c.

2. He shall take charge of all drugs, medicines, clothing, and stores supplied for the use of the infirmary, and shall not issue any drugs or medicines without the directions of the medical officer.

Orders for removal to and from infirmary.

3. He shall paste in a guard book all orders for removal to the infirmary delivered to him with the prisoners; and shall afterwards note on each order the time at which the prisoner shall return to his ward in the prison; for which an order, signed by the medical officer, will always be given to him.

To give notice to medical officer when prisoners are taken worse.

4. If any sick prisoners should appear to be worse, he shall give immediate notice thereof to the medical officer, and take such steps as may appear necessary until he arrives.

To see that the orders of the medical officer are attended.

5. He shall see that the medical officer is treated with proper respect, and that all medicines furnished for the use of the sick are regularly taken, and that the sick prisoners conform in every respect to the directions given by the medical officer. He shall also keep a book, called the "Infirmary Order Book," for the entry of such orders and instructions as may be issued by the inspector or governor, on matters connected with discipline in the infirmary.

Table of diet.

6. He shall carry or send down the diet table, on which the medical officer shall have entered the different allowances for sick prisoners, in the evening of every day, to the steward, in order that he may know what to provide on the next day.

To see that the prisoners are clean in their persons.
To make out washing bills.

7. He shall see that the prisoners in the infirmary are clean in their persons; that every prisoner has clean sheets, at least once a fortnight, and clean linen and stockings (if not required oftener) every Sunday morning. He shall make out a bill of all articles sent to the wash, and shall deliver such articles, together with a duplicate of the bill, to the steward. Upon receiving back any articles from the wash he shall examine them, in order to ascertain whether all the articles mentioned in the bill are returned, and shall report to the steward the deficiency, if any.

To attend to the cleanliness of the infirmary, &c.

8. He shall particularly attend to the cleanliness of every part of the infirmary, and shall see that the surgery is kept clean and in good order. He shall also keep such lights burning during the night as the governor or medical officer shall direct; and shall, when required, aid in attending on the sick, and in the other duties connected with the infirmary; and shall act as clerk to the medical officer.

To keep report book.

9. He shall keep a "Report Book," in which he shall daily note for the information of the governor all occurrences of importance in the infirmary, such as want of repairs, any damage or deficiency, and by whom occasioned, the misconduct of any prisoner, any irregularity in the supply of provisions, &c.

Not to bring certain articles into infirmary.

10. He shall not allow any newspaper or book or other publication into the infirmary which is not the property of the prison, and included in the list of books sanctioned by the prison authorities.

To take care that the prisoners do not partake of his provisions.

11. He shall take care that none of the prisoners partake of the provisions brought in for his own use, and must be cautious to keep such provisions, and in particular beer or other liquor, out of their reach.

To attend to the directions of the governor, &c.

12. He shall conform to all such directions as he shall receive from the director, inspector, and governor in regard to the instruction and moral conduct of the prisoners; shall

shall see that the chaplains are treated in the infirmary with proper deference and respect; and shall give them notice without delay of the visit of any prisoner to have the immediate attendance of the chaplain of the religious persuasion to which he belongs.

13. He shall take care that all bottles, rum, braces, &c., received in the surgery from the storekeeper are returned to him when emptied, and that all bottles, &c., issued to sick prisoners or officers are returned to the surgery; and for this purpose he shall keep a regular bottle account.

14. The place of the infirmary warder, in the event of his absence, shall be supplied by some other officer to be named by the governor, with the concurrence of the medical officer.

15. In the event of his time not being fully occupied in the performance of the duties hereinbefore stated he shall be liable to perform such other reasonable duties as the inspector or governor may require.

THE GATE-KEEPER.

1. The gate-keeper at the entrance to the prison shall have the charge of the keys of the gates, and shall unlock them in the morning for the admission of the officers and servants, and persons authorised to enter, and lock them for the night, at such hours as the governor shall from time to time direct. He shall not leave his post without written permission from the governor, except at such stated times daily as he may be relieved by another officer, for the purpose of taking his meals, &c. He shall endeavour, by every means in his power, to prevent the embezzlement of any of the prison property, or the admission of improper or prohibited articles; for which purpose he may examine all articles carried in or out of the prison; and he may stop any person suspected of bringing in spirits or other prohibited articles for the prisoners, or if illegally carrying out any property belonging to the prison; giving immediate notice thereof to the chief warder or to the governor.

2. He shall not allow any subordinate officer or servant attached to the prison to pass out through the gate during the hours of duty without authority from the governor. He shall keep a list of all subordinate officers or servants residing in the prison who shall go out on leave, in order to know whether they return at the proper time.

3. He shall not permit any person, not being an officer or servant of the prison, or not known to be employed on a workman, or to have business with the steward, to enter the gates without an order from the governor, or other separate authority. In case of doubt as to the order being genuine, or properly obtained, he shall apply to the governor or chief warder before allowing admission.

4. He shall make such daily and other reports of persons passing through the gate as the governor may require; and shall enter in a book the risks of any persons allowed to visit prisoners, with their names, and the time that they remained in the prison.

5. He shall not allow any prisoner to be passed out through the gate except in strict accordance with such instructions in this respect as he may receive from time to time from the governor.

6. He shall observe, on their going out and returning, all prisoners who may have been taken out through the front gate for work, &c., and report immediately anything irregular with respect to them that he may thus discover.

7. He shall be watchful to prevent the escape of prisoners; and it will be his duty to observe closely the appearance of workmen, carters, or other strangers passing out through his gate, in order to detect any attempt on the part of a prisoner to escape in disguise. He shall have authority to stop and search any person whom he may have cause to suspect of making such attempt, and he may also stop any cart or other vehicle.

8. In case of alarm by day or night, he shall communicate immediately with the military guard, if any, at the entrance gate, and also with the warders in the quarters within the prison, and, if necessary, shall ring the alarm bell.

9. When prisoners are employed for any purpose in the vicinity of his gate, he shall keep an eye on their movements, and immediately report any irregularity that he may observe in their conduct.

10. He will comply with all orders which may from time to time be laid down for his guidance by the director, inspector, or governor, and while not required at the gate he will perform such other duties as the governor may direct.

COOK.

1. The cook shall manage the cooking for the whole prison, and will be held responsible for the cleanliness of the kitchen, the coppers, and all utensils in use in the department, as also for the right mixture of all ingredients, and the sufficient boiling of the prisoners' food. He shall every morning receive from the steward note of the number of prisoners to be dieted, with any deviations from the regular diet, either in addition or reduction, that may have been ordered in particular cases; and shall keep such account of quantities received or expended as may be required. He shall be as exact as possible in measuring or weighing the provisions to be served out at each meal to the prisoners; and it shall be his duty immediately to report to the chief warder and steward any defect that he may observe in the quality of the articles of food.

He shall carefully look as, and keep off the reach of the prisoners, food of any description, which they might otherwise be tempted to take; and he is strictly forbidden to employ any prisoner in the cook-house, unless authorised by the governor to do so, and he is on no account to give to prisoners he may be permitted to employ any food beyond their proper allowance. He shall be responsible for the good conduct of prisoners employed under his charge, and shall not fail to report any irregularity of which any prisoner belonging to the cook-house may be guilty.

2. It shall be his duty to cook for the warders' mess, if required, under such regulations as the governor may appoint.

3. In cases of emergency he shall be liable to be called upon to perform such other duties as the governor may direct.

MESSENGER.

A warder may be selected to act as messenger; his principal duties will be to carry letters, &c., to the directors' office, the various prison contractors, &c. He will be careful to perform such duty with as little delay as possible; and when returning to the prison from the directors' office, or other duty, he will invariably report himself to the governor or to the governor's clerks whether he may or may not have letters for the prison. He shall also perform such other duties in the prison as the inspector and governor may from time to time direct.

NIGHT PATROLS INSIDE THE PRISON.

1. Night patrols shall be selected from among the warders according to the regulations which may from time to time be laid down by the inspector or governor. They shall ordinarily be selected from among the second-class warders, but all warders shall be liable to perform such duties.

2. Their duties will be to patrol constantly during their tour of duty the wards or other parts of the prison in which they may be posted, and to attend to all lights and fires ordered to be kept in the prison during the night. They shall be responsible for the order and regularity of the parts of the prison in which they may be posted, and for the safe custody and good conduct of the prisoners confined therein; they will at once repress any disorder or irregularity which may arise, and, if necessary, report such at once to the officer in charge of the prison guard, for which purpose they shall be provided with proper means of communicating with him, or with the night watchmen outside.

The details of their duties will be laid down from time to time by the governor; and when on duty they shall always be in possession of a copy of the instructions and orders which have been issued for their guidance.

3. They shall also perform such special duties by day as the governor may direct, and shall conform to the general rules and regulations of the prison.

NIGHT WATCHMEN.

1. They shall patrol in and about such parts of the prison and premises as may be directed, during such hours and at such intervals throughout the night as may from time to time be appointed; and shall obey the orders and regulations connected with their duties, which may be established by the governor. Their patrolling must be performed without unnecessary noise. They shall vigilantly watch to prevent the escape of any prisoner, and be most careful to attend to any signal or alarm given by any officer on patrol inside the prison; and shall be responsible for the security of the prison during the night. They shall not, on any account or under any pretence whatever, communicate with any prisoner, or enter, without special instructions, such parts of the buildings as may

may be occupied by the prisoners; but in the event of any irregularity or extraordinary occurrence, they shall immediately make a report thereof to the officer in charge of the prison guard, who will communicate with the chief warder or governor if necessary.

2. In case of fire or other emergency, they shall instantly communicate with the officer in charge of the prison guard, and call the governor, and take such other steps as may appear necessary or may be directed by the governor.

3. They shall also perform such special duties by day as the governor may direct, and they shall conform to the general rules and regulations of the prison.

4. All warders shall be liable to be called on to act as night watchmen, but ordinarily the duties will be performed by an officer or officers specially appointed for such duties.

WARDER IN CHARGE OF NIGHT GUARDS.

He shall have the general superintendence of the night watchmen outside and inside the prison, and be responsible that the orders given to those officers are strictly carried out; in event of his observing any suspicious or unusual occurrence, or such being reported to him, he shall at once communicate to the governor and chief warder, and also inform the serjeant of the military guard, if any. He shall frequently visit the hospital and grounds during the night, and shall several times nightly communicate with the watchman on duty in the female prison grounds.

As the hours for his duties, and the duties themselves, may vary from time to time, he will be always furnished with a copy of the routine of his duties, hours, &c., signed by the governor.

All first-class warders are liable to be called on to perform this duty, but ordinarily it will be performed by several selected first-class warders, who will take the duty in turn for a week at a time.

GENERAL RULES FOR SUBORDINATE OFFICERS.

1. The appointment of officers or servants will not be made to any particular prison, but to the convict service generally, and they will be liable to be removed from one convict prison to another, for the benefit of the service, at the discretion of the directors.

2. The appointment of all subordinate officers and servants shall be held on probation for the first six months, during which period they shall be liable to be discharged from the service on receiving one fortnight's notice or pay, should they be found in any respect unsuited for the due and satisfactory performance of the duties required of them. The appointment of a subordinate officer or servant shall not be confirmed on the expiration of his probation unless his conduct, character, temper, and abilities have proved in all respects satisfactory.

3. It is provided by the 6 & 7 Vict. c. 26, s. 22: Every person who shall rescue any convict either during the time of his conveyance to or from the prison, or of his imprisonment therein, and also every person who shall aid in any such rescue, shall be guilty of felony; and every person having the custody of any such convict, or being employed by the person having such custody as a keeper, under-keeper, turnkey, assistant, or guard, who shall knowingly and wilfully allow such convict to escape, and also every person who, by supplying arms, tools, or instruments of disguise or otherwise, shall in any manner aid any such convict in any attempts to escape, though no escape be actually made, and every person who shall attempt to rescue any such convict or aid in any such attempt, though no rescue be actually made, shall be found guilty of felony; and every person, having such custody as aforesaid, who shall carelessly allow any such convict to escape, shall be guilty of misdemeanour, and, being lawfully convicted of such misdemeanour, shall be liable to fine or imprisonment, or to both, at the discretion of the court.

4. All officers and servants will be held responsible for being fully acquainted with the rules and orders relating to their respective duties. They shall strictly conform to and obey the orders of the director, inspector, governor, and all their superior officers. They shall assist them in maintaining order and discipline among the prisoners. For this end punishment for prison offences must sometimes be resorted to upon their report; but good temper and good example on the part of the officers and servants will have great influence in preventing the frequent recurrence of offences, and the necessity for such punishments.

5. It is the duty of all officers to treat the prisoners with kindness and humanity, and to listen patiently to and report their complaints or grievances, being firm, at the same time, in maintaining order and discipline, and enforcing complete observance of the rules and regulations of the establishment.

The great object of reclaiming the criminal should always be kept in view by every officer in the prison; and they should strive to acquire a moral influence over the prisoners, by performing their duties conscientiously, but without harshness. They should especially try to raise the prisoners' minds to a proper feeling of moral obligation by the example of their own uniform regard to truth and integrity even in the smallest matters. Such conduct will, in most cases, ensure the respect and confidence of prisoners, and will make the duties of the officers more satisfactory to themselves, and more useful to the public.

Not to strike a prisoner.

6. Officers or servants shall not strike a prisoner except compelled to do so in self-defence, or at any time use more force than may be absolutely necessary in the execution of their duty.

To inform the authorities of the moral state of the prisoners.

7. The officers shall carefully observe the character and habits and industry of the prisoners under their charge; and it being of the utmost importance that the authorities shall be fully informed on these points, the several officers shall carefully and impartially keep such records as may be ordered, and shall consider it to be their duty to afford at all times unreserved information on such subjects.

To report misconduct of prisoners to the governor.
Not to punish prisoners.

8. No subordinate officer or servant, on any pretence whatever, through favour, or mistaken notions of kindness, shall fail to make an immediate report to the governor, or other superior officer, of any misconduct or wilful disobedience of the prison regulations. No subordinate officer shall take upon himself to punish any prisoner, unless ordered by the governor.

Officers and servants to preserve silence when required by regulations, and watch the prisoners carefully.

9. The prisoners when in association shall be placed under the control and superintendence of officers, whose duty is shall be to enforce silence in all cases wherein the regulations require it, and to prevent all improper communication in those cases in which prisoners are allowed the privilege of communicating. They shall carefully watch the prisoners in their various movements and employments, and use the utmost alacrity and vigilance to prevent escape.

Officers and servants not to be familiar with prisoners.

10. No subordinate officer or servant of the prison shall unnecessarily converse with a prisoner, or allow any familiarity on the part of prisoners towards any other officer or servant of the prison, or on any account speak of any matter of discipline or prison duties or arrangements in the hearing of prisoners.

Counting parties of prisoners.

11. On all occasions the officer who receives charge of a party of prisoners will count the number of prisoners therein, and report the number dealt to the officer from whom he received them, after which the officer in charge shall be held responsible for their safe custody and regular conduct, and especially that they do not struggle or hold unauthorized communication with each other, or with any unauthorized persons, or in any way get possession of prohibited articles.

Directed for improper conduct.

12. All officers placed in authority over prisoners, and all persons employed in the prison, must be persons of moral principles and established character; any disreputable conduct even outside the prison will render an officer or servant liable to dismissal. Improper language, incurring debts which they are unable to pay, or keeping bad company, will be considered sufficient ground for the discontinuance of the services of officers or other persons employed in the prison.

Officers to attend divine service.

13. All officers, assistants, and servants of the prison shall punctually attend divine service with the prisoners, unless on duty, or excused by the governor; their absence and the cause thereof, to be entered in the governor's journal.

To treat their superiors with respect.

14. The subordinate officers and servants of the prison shall at all times treat their superiors with respect. They shall see that the prisoners are industrious at all times, and that no disrespect is shown by the prisoners to the officers or persons employed in other departments.

Officers' uniform.

15. All subordinate officers shall pay strict attention to cleanliness of person and dress and shall at all times, within, or in the vicinity of the prison, wear a plain uniform; they shall not, either in the prison or without, wear any part of their uniform with plain clothes; they shall dress either entirely in uniform or in plain clothes, and farther, shall conform to such regulations concerning their personal appearance as may be established.

Restrictions as to time and place of attendance.

16. No subordinate officer or servant shall be absent during his regular hours of attendance, without permission of the inspector or governor in writing. Subordinate officers and servants are to confine themselves, while within the walls, to their respective posts, unless when they have occasion to go to any other part of the establishment, in obedience to the orders of the governor, or in the performance of any special duty. They shall not, however, be considered exclusively connected with that part of the prison to which they more particularly belong, but shall be liable to be employed in any other part, at the discretion of the governor.

Keys.

17. No officer or servant entrusted with keys shall take them out of the prison, leave them lying about, or lend them to another on any pretence whatever, but shall, when leaving the prison or coming off duty on any occasion, deliver his keys to such officer as
  may

may be authorised to receive them; taking from such officer an acknowledgment, without which he shall not be allowed to quit the prison.

18. No subordinate officer or servant shall be permitted to receive any visitors in the interior of the prison without the sanction of the governor; and all such officers and servants not resident in the prison, are required to live within such limits as shall be from time to time laid down.

Subordinate officers not to receive visitors.

Non-resident officers to live within prescribed limits.

19. No officer or servant of the prison shall sell, nor shall any person in trust for him, or employed by him, sell, or have any benefit or advantage from the sale of, any article to any prisoner; or let, or have the interest or advantage from the loan or letting of, any article to, or have any pecuniary dealing whatsoever with, any prisoner, or employ any prisoner on any private errand; or correspond with or hold any intercourse with the friends or relatives of any prisoner, or make any unauthorised communication concerning the prison to any person whatsoever.

No officers to have dealings with prisoners, or any concern in or advantage from loans, &c.

20. The 17 & 18 Vict. c. 76, directs that: Every officer or servant of the establishment who shall bring in or carry out, or endeavour to bring in or carry out, or knowingly allow to be brought in or carried out, to or for any prisoner, any money, clothing, provisions, tobacco, letters, papers, or other articles whatsoever not allowed by the rules of the prison, shall be forthwith suspended from his office by the governor of the prison, who shall report the offence to a Director, who upon proof of the offence may cause the offender to be apprehended and carried before a Justice of the Peace, who shall be empowered to hear and determine any such offence in a summary way; and every such officer or servant, upon conviction of such offence before a Justice of the Peace, shall be liable to pay a penalty not exceeding 50 l., or, in the discretion of the Justice, to be imprisoned in the common gaol or house of correction, there to be kept, with or without hard labour, for any time not exceeding six calendar months.

Bringing in or carrying out unauthorised articles.

21. No officer or servant of the prison shall directly or indirectly, have any interest in any contract or agreement for the supply of the prison; or receive directly or indirectly, under any pretence whatsoever, any fee, or gratuity, or present, from any constructor, or person tendering for any contract with the establishment, nor from any prisoner or prisoner's friend, nor from any person visiting the prison.

No officer to have any interest in contracts, or to receive fees from contractors, &c.

22. No subordinate officer or servant shall use spirituous liquors or tobacco within the prison walls, except under such restrictions as to time and place as may be laid down by the governor, and approved by a Director; or shall on any account whatever bring into the wards or rooms occupied by prisoners, tobacco, snuff, or tobacco pipes; any infraction of this rule to be invariably reported to the Directors.

Use of tobacco or spirituous liquors.

23. The subordinate officers living in the prison shall, with such exceptions as special duties may render necessary, mess within the prison. The senior officer present is expected to be present before and after dinner, and is responsible for due order and regularity in the mess room. Officers or servants messing together are required, both for their own comfort and the respectability of the establishment, to be particularly observant of habits of decorum, morality, and order, and are strictly prohibited from gambling and card-playing. Hours of meals, under ordinary circumstances, will be one hour for dinner and half an hour each for breakfast and tea, at such times as may be directed. No officer shall continue in the mess-room, or the sitting room of the quarters within the prison wall, after ten o'clock at night, except when placed there on duty, and all subordinate officers and servants except those on night duty, are to retire to bed at that time.

Officers messing.

24. All wrangling or disputes between officers of the prison are strictly prohibited. Any question connected with points of duty must be referred, at a convenient time, for the decision of the chief or principal warden, or, if necessary, to the governor; and all complaints by one subordinate officer or servant against another must be made in writing to the governor. Such report must be delivered within 24 hours of the occurrence complained of or it will not be received; and if it should be found that any such complaints are frivolous or vexatious, or arise from a spirit of ill-dealing, malice, or revenge, it is to be entered in the "Officers' Misconduct Book" and a full report made to a Director.

Grievances or complaints, how to be settled.

And subordinate officer or servant having any grievance connected with his duty or situation in the prison must state the same respectfully in writing for the governor's decision, or, if necessary, for appeal to higher authority; any other proceeding on the part of an officer or servant for this purpose will render him liable to dismissal, or such minor penalty as the case may deserve. Any discussion or other proceeding with a view to, or tending to, or in the nature of, a combination among officers or servants for any object connected with their duties or position in the prison, unless with the cognizance and sanction of the governor, are strictly prohibited, and every officer or servant joining therein will be liable to dismissal or other punishment according to the degree of his offence. All wrangling or discussion about private matters between officers and servants within the prison or elsewhere, while on duty, is also strictly forbidden; and they must be careful to avoid, as much as possible, speaking about or discussing any of the arrangements of, or occurrences that may take place within the prison, with any person not connected with the establishment.

To state grievances respectfully.

Unnecessary talk on duty prohibited.

Fines and their fund.

24. Fines may be levied by the governor on the subordinate officers and servants for neglect or violation of duty, according to his discretion, but no fine above 3s. shall be levied without the sanction of a Director. All fines and remissions will be entered in the officers' misconduct book, which the governor is required to keep; and the final fund will be administered and distributed for the general benefit of officers and servants and their families, as may be from time to time directed by the Directors; but no officer or servant shall be deemed to have any claim whatever on the fund as a matter of right. Subordinate officers may also be punished for breach of prison rules, neglect or violation of duty, or other misconduct, by being reduced to a lower place on the list of officers holding the same rank, according to circumstances, or in such other manner as may be approved by the Directors, or they may, by order or approval of the Chief Secretary, be reduced to a lower rank and pay.

An inspector may fine a subordinate officer in any sum not exceeding 10s.; but all cases of suspension must be invariably referred to a Director.

No officer or servant to be fined for neglect of duty without having an opportunity of making any explanation he may wish to offer.

26. No officer or servant shall be fined or subjected to any penalty for neglect of duty or misconduct of any description, except being late for duty, without being called on to state in writing any explanation he may have to offer relative thereto, and such document shall be filed in the governor's office.

Officers or servants dismissed, &c.

27. Subordinate officers or servants, whose services are discontinued (except such as are temporarily engaged, or who have not completed their probation, or are at weekly wages, or shall be dismissed for misconduct), shall be entitled to a month's notice or a month's pay.

To give up their quarters at dismissal, &c.
Not to leave their service without giving notice.

28. Officers who may be dismissed, or discharged, or who may resign their appointment, are required forthwith to give up the quarters they may have occupied.

Subordinate officers or servants (except those in temporary employment, or otherwise described in Article No. 27), leaving without a month's previous notice in writing, or who shall so misconduct themselves as to render their immediate suspension and subsequent dismissal, shall be liable, by order of the Board of Directors, to forfeit a sum not exceeding one month's pay. Those excepted as above shall be liable to a forfeiture of a week's pay, under similar circumstances.

Officers or servants disabled from duty by sickness.

29. Any subordinate officer or servant disabled from the regular performance of duty by illness must give or send immediate notice to the governor and to the medical officer. The governor shall have power to grant sick leave upon the report of the medical officer for any time not exceeding one week. The sick leave may be renewed weekly upon a further similar report, but that at the end of one month (reckoned from the date of the first leave) the officer or servant has not resumed his duty, and is not in health to perform it otherwise, his place shall be supplied by another person, and the sick officer or servant removed from the pay of the establishment, unless under special authority. A subordinate officer or servant returning to duty from the sick list, must have the report of the medical officer of his fitness to undertake it. Subordinate officers and servants on the sick list (unless they are suffering from accidents received on duty), are not necessarily entitled to rations, and shall not be allowed to draw them, unless they shall be treated in the prison infirmary. Officers going on the sick list after giving in their resignations shall receive no pay for such periods, unless their sickness is caused by accidents occurring on duty. Subordinate officers or servants who may be suspended from duty, and afterwards restored to their situation, shall not receive any pay for the time during which they shall have been suspended, unless a special order shall be given to that effect. Any subordinate officer or servant, who in the course of one year shall have been in the aggregate more than 60 days absent from duty on account of sickness (except in consequence of accidents received on duty), and others who may not be in health to perform their duty properly, shall be examined and reported upon by the medical officer, and their cases laid before the Directors, who, unless there appear strong reasons for the contrary, will recommend them to the Chief Secretary for discharge.

But in all cases (those excepted in which the medical officer certifies, in writing, that it will be injurious to health, or much retard recovery), subordinate officers shall invariably be treated in the prison hospital.

30. No officer shall on any account enter a prisoner's cell at night unless accompanied by another officer, and then only in case of the prisoner's sickness or other emergency.

Officers relieved from duty to instruct their successor.

31. All officers or servants on being relieved from any particular duty, or transferred to another part of the prison, shall point out to their successors all matters of special importance connected with their duties, and explain any directions of the governor, medical officer, or other superior officer, affecting any particular prisoner.

Prevention against secreting improper articles.

32. All officers and servants shall be watchful to detect and prevent any person secreting prohibited articles for the prisoners about the prison, and shall immediately report any such occurrence. They shall especially guard against clothes being left lying about in places accessible to the prisoners, and shall report at the earliest opportunity any suspicious circumstance of this kind, or the loitering of improper or suspicious persons that they may observe about the prison.

34. Officers in charge of wards or other parts of the prison are to set cleaners to work in the halls, cells, passages, &c., and cleaners are always to be required, after work, to produce the brushes, brooms, &c., with which they may have been furnished. The officers shall expedite this necessary work, so that it may be completed at the time fixed by the governor. Especial care must be taken that no ladders, planks, wheelbarrows, ropes, chains, implements, or materials of any kind likely to facilitate escape, are left unnecessarily exposed at any time in the yards, ward, or elsewhere. All such articles when not in use must be kept in their appointed places. Every officer or servant is bound to report immediately any instance of such articles being left in neglect of this rule, whether is occurs in his own department of the prison or otherwise. *(margin: Prisoners to be employed in cleaning, &c. Ladders, &c., to be left in their proper places.)*

35. Leave of absence, not exceeding 14 days in each year, will be ordinarily granted to each of the subordinate officers of the prison. Leave, however, shall not be claimed as a right, nor will it be granted except as an indulgence to officers whose conduct shall, in all respects, be perfectly satisfactory; and then only at such periods, and under such restrictions, as a due regard to the interests and efficiency of the service will admit. No deduction will be made from the pay of officers to whom leave may be granted under the foregoing rule; but reliefs will not be found for such officers. *(margin: Leave of absence.)*

SCALE OF FINES.

Fines may be levied by the governor upon all the subordinate officers and servants of the establishment for neglect of duty. Such fines to be disposed of as may from time to time be directed by the Directors.

1. Coming into duty any time not exceeding five minutes; each offence, 3 d., and 2 d. for each additional five minutes.

2. Leaving a cell or principal door unlocked.

3. Entering a prisoner's cell at night contrary to orders.

4. Allowing any unauthorised person to communicate with a prisoner within or outside the prison walls.

5. Leaving prisoners in the halls, wards, prison grounds, exercising yards, or elsewhere within or outside the prison walls, unattended by an officer or other authorised person.

6. Cursing, swearing, or using indecent or immoral language.

7. Allowing to be lying about in the part of the prison under their charge or superintendence, ladders or anything likely to facilitate the escape of a prisoner.

8. Sleeping whilst on duty—by day.
1st offence, 3 s.; 2nd offence, 5 s.; third offence, suspension.

9. Leaving a cell, or passage, or other door singly locked, which ought to be double shotted.

10. Leaving a passage or other door (not included in No. 9) unlocked.

11. Leaving keys in a door or lying about.
1st offence, 3 s.; 2nd offence, 4 s.; 3rd offence, 5 s.

12. Sleeping whilst on duty—by night, suspension.

13. Omitting at the proper time to ring the signal or call-bell, should there be one.

14. Speaking unnecessarily of the prison arrangements in the hearing of prisoners or in public.

15. Omitting to make the prescribed reports at the proper times, or to keep the prescribed lists, rolls, or accounts.

16. Carelessly searching or omitting to search a prisoner, and allowing him to retain any forbidden article or money.

17. Neglecting to report the wish of a prisoner to see a Director, the inspector, governor, chaplain, medical officer, chief or principal warder.

18. Neglecting to extinguish any lights or fires at the times appointed.
First offence 1 s.; second offence 3 s.; third offence, 4 s.

19. Neglecting to have the lights, lamps, candles, &c., properly trimmed and burning at the time appointed.

20. Omitting to pull the tell-tale at the appointed times.

21. Neglecting to answer a prisoner's call or bell.

22. Neglecting

22. Neglecting to examine the cell or other fastenings under their charge, and to examine and search the wards, cells, building, &c.

23. Allowing tools or other materials, or any cleaning utensils, to be lying about out of their appointed places.

24. Allowing dirt to accumulate in the wards, cells, yards, or passages, or other places under their charge.

25. Neglecting to attend to the cleanliness of the prisoners in their charge, or the necessary repairs of their clothing.

26. Omitting to report any injury done to the prison furniture, or any marks or defacings on the walls, windows, partitions, or paint, or other portions of the prison under their charge or superintendence.

27. Allowing prisoners to leave the wards or cells improperly dressed.

28. Inattention when in charge of prisoners in the wards or when at labour or exercise, &c.

29. Communicating with unauthorised persons in the prison or outside when in charge of prisoners.

30. Omitting to give notice in writing to the governor, or appointed officer, previously to leaving the prison on leave of absence.

31. Allowing strangers to enter the wards, sheds, or exercising yards when occupied by prisoners, unless by order of the Directors, the governor, or other competent authority.

32. Appearing in or outside the prison improperly dressed, slovenly, unshaven or unclean.

33. Appearing at any time, without permission, within the prison or beyond the prison walls, out of uniform.

34. Being absent from quarters after the hour appointed at night without special leave.

35. Wrangling together, whether on duty or not, or in any way obstructing the duties of the prison.

36. Omitting to report without delay any irregularity or omission of duty on their own part or that of any officer, or servant, or a prisoner.
1st offence, 1 s.; 2nd offence, 1 s. 6 d.; 3rd offence, 2 s.

37. Omitting when sick to send or deliver a medical certificate or notice to the governor, or omitting when convalescent to report his return (in writing) before 10 o'clock on the day of such return.
1st offence, 9 d.; 2nd offence, 1 s. 6 d., 3rd offence, 3 s.

38. Omitting to escort the prisoners going to and returning from work or exercise, and at locking up and unlocking, or other appointed times.

39. Omitting at any time to withdraw from the halls, yards, shops, wards, or cells, such tools, implements, and articles as ought to be withdrawn.

40. Making unnecessary noises in or about the prison.
1st offence, 6 d.; 2nd offence, 1 s.; 3rd offence, 1 s. 6 d.

COOK.

41. Serving more or less than the prisoners' proper allowance of food.

42. Inattention to the cooking of the officers' or prisoners' meals, or negligently spoiling the same.

43. Neglecting to keep such accounts of provisions, &c., as may be required of him, or immediately to report any deficiency in the quality of the provisions.

44. Omitting to prepare the meals at the appointed times, whether for officer or prisoners.

45. Neglecting to keep the kitchen, store-rooms, or other parts of the prison under his charge, together with the furniture and utensils therein, in clean condition and good order.
1st offence, 1 s. 6 d.; 2nd offence, 3 s.; 3rd offence, 4 s.

GATE-KEEPER.

ALL SUBORDINATE OFFICERS and SERVANTS.

42. Disobedience or negligence with respect to any of the prison rules or regulations not here expressly mentioned, or to any order given by their superior officers or persons in authority connected with the prison.

For each offence, any sum not less than 6 d., nor exceeding 1 s. 6 d.; second offence, double; 3rd offence, treble.

The repetition of an offence will not be deemed a second or third offence under this scale, unless occurring within six months of the previous offence. Any offence repeated beyond the third time will be specially reported for the consideration of the Directors, except cases of being late for duty, which will be specially reported whenever the governor may consider it necessary.

Fines exceeding 3 s. and not exceeding 10 s. can be imposed by order of the Inspector.

A Director shall have the power to fine any subordinate officers for neglect or violation of duty; in no case to exceed one month's pay of the officer fined. If in his judgment a greater punishment is required, a representation must be made to the Government with a view to the officer's being recommended for dismissal.

BY THE GENERAL PRISONS BOARD FOR IRELAND.

In pursuance of the General Prisons (Ireland) Act, 1877, the General Prisons Board for Ireland hereby make the following rules for the government of convict prisons in Ireland:—

RULES FOR DEPUTY GOVERNORS.

1. He shall constantly reside at the prison, and thoroughly acquaint himself with all the rules.

He is on no pretence whatever to absent himself from the prison without leave from the governor; and is on no instance to be absent at the same time with the governor.

2. He shall be the assistant to the governor on all occasions, and carry into effect his instructions. During the governor's absence or inability to attend to his duties from illness the charge of the prison shall be entrusted to him, and he shall then have all the powers stated in printed rules, and be required to perform all the duties of the governor; but he is on no account whatever to alter or suspend any regulations established by the governor for the internal government of the prison. He shall in his general conduct and in the discharge of his duties conform to the rules laid down for the guidance of the governor, and he shall see that the governor's orders are strictly obeyed.

3. He shall visit the several working parties at such times as the governor shall direct, and see that the prisoners are kept steadily to their labour. He shall diligently observe the behaviour of all the subordinate officers and servants as well as of the prisoners. He shall see that they strictly adhere to the rules, and shall report immediately to the governor any neglect or misconduct that may come to his knowledge.

4. He shall attend parades, the unlock and lockup of the prison, and perform such office and other duties as the governor may from time to time direct.

5. He is at all times to be on the alert to prevent or counteract escape, and to make himself well acquainted with the rules and regulations of the prison.

He is to make the governor immediately acquainted with any misconduct of the officers, or any irregularity or violation of the rules of the prison; also with any complaint made by the prisoners.

AMENDED RULES FOR CHAPLAINS.

Rule No. 10 for the chaplains of convict prisons is hereby repealed, and the following rule is substituted for it:—

"The General Prisons Board may, upon the application of any chaplain, approve of certain clergymen, not exceeding three in number, of the same religious persuasion as such chaplain, from whom he may appoint a substitute or substitutes, or except assistance under the circumstances, and in the case hereinafter provided.

"The chaplain shall insert the name and residence of the clergymen so approved of in the Chaplain's Journal.

"The chaplain, when he is absent on leave, or when from sickness or other sufficient cause, he is prevented from performing his duties in person, may nominate one or more of the clergymen so approved of as his substitute or substitutes, or may accept the assistance of any of the said clergymen in performance of his duties.

"The General Prisons Board may withdraw an approval given under this rule."

RULE FOR ASSISTANT CHAPLAINS.

It shall be his duty to assist, to the best of his power, in the clerical and other duties prescribed under the head "Chaplain," and consider himself as standing in the relation of curate to that officer. In the event of any difference of opinion between the chaplain and the assistant chaplain upon the subject of arrangement of duties, the case is to be referred to the General Prisons Board.

ALTERATION OF RULES RESPECTING ANNUAL REPORTS.

Rule No. 10 for the Directors of Convict Prisons is hereby repealed, and the following rule is substituted for it :—

The General Prisons Board shall, at such time or times as the Lord Lieutenant may appoint, make a report or reports to the Lord Lieutenant of the condition of the prisons and prisoners within their jurisdiction, and with respect to the registration of criminals; and an annual report to be made by them with respect to every prison within their jurisdiction shall be laid before both Houses of Parliament.

Such report shall include a yearly return of all punishments of any kind which may have been inflicted within each prison, and the offences for which such punishments were inflicted.

So much of the following rules, viz. :—

    Rule No. 45 for governors,
    Rule No. 54 for superintendents,
    Rule No. 16 for chaplains,
    Rule No. 29 for medical officers of female prison,
    Rule No. 30 for medical officers of male prison,

as require that the Annual Reports of these officers shall be submitted on or before the 10th day of January in each year, is hereby repealed, and these officers shall hereafter submit such Annual Reports as they are required to make by aforementioned rules, respectively, at such time in each year as may be fixed by the General Prisons Board.

The foregoing rules shall apply to the several convict prisons in Ireland, and shall come into operation upon the expiration of 40 days after the same, having been settled and approved by the Lord Lieutenant and Privy Council, shall have been laid before Parliament.

Made and executed this 14th day of July 1884, by "The General Prisons Board for Ireland."

(SEAL.)   (signed)   W. F. O'Brien,
                              Vice-Chairman.

By the Lord Lieutenant and Privy Council in Ireland.

Carnarvon,

In pursuance of the General Prisons (Ireland) Act, 1877, We, the Lord Lieutenant-General and General Governor of Ireland, with the approval, advice, and consent of the Privy Council in Ireland, have settled and hereby approve of the foregoing Rules made by the General Prisons Board for Ireland.

Given at the Council Chamber, Dublin Castle,
this 29th day of July 1885.

Ashbourne, C.
W. H. F. Cogan.
M. Morris.
Hedges Eyre Chatterton.
Thomas Steele, General.

SCALES of DIETARY for Convicts in Public Works Convict Prisons.

For Prisoners on the Ordinary Prison Diet (Labour Class).—See Form B.

For Prisoners committed to Cells whilst their cases are awaiting decision, and for Prisoners in Separate Confinement for special reasons.

MEAL.	DAY.	DESCRIPTION.		QUANTITY.
Breakfast	Daily	Oatmeal Rice Milk	} Made into Stir- about.	
Dinner	Sunday Tuesday Thursday Saturday	Bread Soup		
	Monday Wednesday Friday	Bread Milk		
Supper	Sunday Tuesday Thursday Saturday	Bread		
	Monday Wednesday Friday	Bread Milk		

For Prisoners on the Invalid Diet.

MEAL.	DAY.	DESCRIPTION.		QUANTITY.
Breakfast	Sunday Tuesday Thursday	Coffee Chicory Molasses Milk Bread	} Made into 1 pint of Coffee.	
	Monday Wednesday Friday Saturday	Oatmeal Rice Milk	} Made into Stir- about.	
Dinner	Sunday	Oatmeal Rice Vegetables Beef Pea meal	} Made into 1 pint of Soup.	
	Monday Wednesday Friday Saturday	Bread Milk		
	Tuesday Thursday	Oatmeal Rice Vegetables Beef Bread	} Made into 1 pint of Soup.	
Supper	Daily	Bread Milk		

(A.)—Scale of Dietary for Convicts in Public Works Convict Prisons—continued.

For Prisoners in Penal Class.

MEAL.	DAY.	DESCRIPTION.	QUANTITY.
Breakfast	Sunday, Tuesday, Thursday, Saturday	Oatmeal } Made into Stirabout { Rice, Milk	8 oz. 3 oz. ½ pint.
	Monday, Wednesday, Friday	Oatmeal } Made into Stirabout { Rice, Milk	8½ oz. 2½ oz. 1 pint.
Dinner	Sunday, Tuesday, Thursday, Saturday	Bread, Milk	½ lb. ½ pint.
	Monday, Wednesday, Friday	Bread, Milk	1 lb. 1 pint.
Supper	Sunday, Tuesday, Thursday, Saturday	Bread, Milk	½ lb. ½ pint.
	Monday, Wednesday, Friday	Bread, Milk	½ lb. ½ pint.

(B.)

ORDINARY DIET (Labour Class).

DAY.	BREAKFAST.	DINNER.	SUPPER.
Sundays	8 oz. Oatmeal, 3 oz. Rice, 1 oz. Indian Meal, ½ pint Milk, 5 oz. Bread } Made into Stirabout	5 oz. Oatmeal, 3 oz. Rice, 3 oz. Vegetables, ½ lb. Beef, 20 lb. Potatoes } Made into one pint of Soup.	1 lb. bread, 1 oz. Coffee, 1 oz. Sugar, 1 pint Milk } Made into one pint of Coffee.
Monday, Wednesday, Friday	8 oz. Oatmeal, 3 oz. Rice, 1 oz. Indian Meal, ½ pint Milk, 5 oz. Bread } Made into Stirabout	1 lb. Bread, 1 pint Milk	1 lb. bread, 1 oz. Coffee, 1 oz. Sugar, 1 pint Milk } Made into one pint of Coffee.
Tuesday, Thursday	8 oz. Oatmeal, 3 oz. Rice, 1 oz. Indian Meal, ½ pint Milk, 5 oz. Bread } Made into Stirabout	5 oz. Oatmeal, 3 oz. Rice, 3 oz. Vegetables, ½ lb. Beef, 20 lb. Potatoes } Made into one pint of Soup.	1 lb. bread, 1 oz. Coffee, 1 oz. Sugar, 1 pint Milk } Made into one pint of Coffee.
Saturday	8 oz. Oatmeal, 3 oz. Rice, 1 oz. Indian Meal, ½ pint Milk, 5 oz. Bread } Made into Stirabout	5 oz. Oatmeal, 3 oz. Rice, 3 oz. Vegetables, ½ lb. Beef, 5 oz. Bread } Made into one pint of Soup.	1 lb. bread, 1 oz. Coffee, 1 oz. Sugar, 1 pint Milk } Made into one pint of Coffee.

NOTE.—Beef is estimated as weighed uncooked, without bone.

General Prisons Board, Dublin Castle, 8 March 1897.   Approved, &c. &c. &c.   Charles F. Bourke, Chairman.

SCALES of DIETARY in Mountjoy Male Convict Prison.

1. Old Classification. 2. New Classification.	REFORMATORY. 1. First Four Months. 2. First Four Months.			ORDINARY. 1. Next Four Months. 2. Next Five Months.		
MEAL	Day.	Description.	Quantity.	Day.	Description.	Quantity.
Breakfast	Daily	Bread - - -	10 oz.	Daily	Bread - - -	10 oz.
		Coffee - - -	1 pint.		Coffee - - -	1 pint.
Dinner	Sunday Thursday	Bread - - -	6 oz.	Sunday Thursday	Bread - - -	6 oz.
		Potatoes - +	1 lb.		Potatoes - -	1 lb.
		Soup (oatmeal) -	1½ pint.		Meat (with bone) -	6 oz.
					Soup - - -	1 pint.
	Monday Friday	Bread - - -	10 oz.	Monday Friday	Bread - - -	10 oz.
		Coffee - - -	1 pint.		Coffee - - -	1 pint.
	Tuesday Saturday	Bread - - -	10 oz.	Tuesday Saturday	Bread - - -	10 oz.
		Soup (oatmeal) -	1½ pint.		Soup (oxhead) -	2½ pint.
	Wednesday	Bread - - -	12 oz.	Wednesday	Bread - - -	10 oz.
		New milk -	½ pint.		New milk -	½ pint.
Supper	Daily	Bread - - -	8 oz.	Daily	Bread - - -	8 oz.
		Cocoa - - -	1 pint.		Cocoa - - -	1 pint.

WORKING.—See Form B.

PUNISHMENT OF BREAD and WATER DIET.—1 lb. bread daily, with water.

Ingredients to Each Ration.

Tea	} To every pint	{ oz. tea, ½ oz. sugar, ⅟₁₂ pint milk.
Coffee		{ oz. coffee, ⅓ oz. chicory, 1 oz. sugar, and ⅓ pint milk.
Cocoa		{ oz. cocoa, ⅓ oz. sugar, and ⅟₁₂ pint milk.
Meat soup	To every pint of the liquor in which the meat is cooked add 2 oz. oatmeal and 6 oz. vegetables, with pepper and salt to taste.
Oxhead soup	To every pint add a half, ⅟₁₂ oatmeal, 6 oz. vegetables, 2 oz. oatmeal, with pepper and salt to taste.

(D.)

SCALES of DIETARY in Mountjoy Female Convict Prison.

No. 1.

1. Old Classification.	1. Probation, Third, and Second Classes.	First 12 Months.
2. New Classification.	2. Probation Class and Third Class, First Three Months.	

Meal.	Day.	Description.	Quantity.
Breakfast	Monday, Tuesday, Wednesday, Friday	Bread, Coffee	8 oz., 1 pint.
	Monday, Thursday, Saturday	Bread, Cocoa	8 oz., 1 pint.
Dinner	Sunday, Monday, Wednesday, Friday, Saturday	Bread, Coffee	12 oz., 1 pint.
	Tuesday, Thursday	Potatoes, Soup, Meat (with bone)	8 lb., 1 pint, 4 oz.
Supper	Daily	Bread, Tea	6 oz., 1 pint.

No. 2.

	1. First Class.	Second 12 Months.
	2. Third Class after First Three Months, and Second Class First Six Months.	

Meal.	Day.	Description.	Quantity.
Breakfast	Sunday, Tuesday, Wednesday, Friday	Bread, Coffee	8 oz., 1 pint.
	Monday, Thursday, Saturday	Bread, Cocoa	6 oz., 1 pint.
	Sunday, Saturday	Bread, Soup	8 oz., 1 pint.
Dinner	Monday, Wednesday, Friday	Bread, Coffee	12 oz., 1 pint.
	Tuesday, Thursday	Potatoes, Soup, Meat (with bone)	8 lb., 1 pint, 6 oz.
Supper	Daily	Bread, Tea	6 oz., 1 pint.

(D.)—Scale of Dietary in Mountjoy Female Convict Prison—continued.

No. 3.

1. Old Classification. 2. New Classification.	1. Advanced Class . . . . 2. Second Class, after First Six Months, and First Class	} Remainder of Sentence.	
Meal.	**Day.**	**Description.**	**Quantity.**
Breakfast - -	Sunday . . . Tuesday . . . Wednesday . . . Friday . . .	Bread . . . Coffee . . .	8 oz. 1 pint.
	Monday . . . Thursday . . . Saturday . . .	Bread . . . Cocoa . . .	8 oz. 1 pint.
Dinner - - -	Sunday . . . Monday . . . Saturday . . .	Bread . . . Soup - .	8 oz. 1 pint.
	Wednesday . . . Friday . . .	Bread . . . Coffee . . .	10 oz. 1 pint.
	Tuesday . . . Thursday . . .	Potatoes . . . Soup . . . Meat (with bone)	9 lb. 1 pint. 6 oz.
Supper - - -	Daily . . .	Bread . . . Tea . . .	4 oz. 1 part.

No. 4.

	First Class.			Bread and Water.
Meal.	**Day.**	**Description.**	**Quantity.**	
Breakfast - -	Sunday . . . Tuesday . . . Wednesday . . . Friday . . .	Bread . . . Coffee . . .	6 oz. 1 pint -	Daily, 1 lb. bread or biscuit, and 1 lb. of dinner, with water.
	Monday . . . Thursday . . . Saturday . . .	Bread . . . Cocoa . . .	6 oz. 1 pint -	
Dinner - -	Sunday . . . Tuesday . . . Wednesday . . . Thursday . . . Friday . . .	Bread . . . Coffee . . .	10 oz. 1 pint -	
	Monday . . . Saturday . . .	Potatoes . . Bread . . . Soup . . .	1 lb. - 6 oz. - 1 pint -	
Supper - -	Daily . . .	Bread . . . Milk gruel . . .	4 oz. 1 pint -	

Ingredients to each Ration.

Tea - - -	} To every pint {{ ¼ oz. tea, ½ oz. sugar, ½ pint milk.
Coffee - - -	½ oz. coffee, ½ oz. sugar, ½ pint milk.
Cocoa - - -	½ oz. cocoa, ½ oz. sugar, ½ pint milk.
Meat soup - -	To every pint of the liquor in which the meat is cooked add 8 oz. vegetables, ½ oz. oatmeal, ½ oz. rice, with pepper and salt to taste.
Shin of beef soup -	To every pint, 6 oz. shin of beef, 8 oz. vegetables, 1 oz. oatmeal, with pepper and salt to taste.
Milk gruel - -	To every pint, 6 oz. oatmeal, and ½ pint milk.

(E.)

SCALE of DIETARY for Convicts in the Intermediate Class.

Day.	Breakfast.	Dinner.	Supper (daily).
Sunday	Tea 1 pint, bread ¼ lb.	Beef, cooked, ½ lb. Soup, 1 pint. Potatoes, 2 lbs. Bread, ¼ lb.	Coffee, 1 pint. Bread, ½ lb.
Monday Tuesday Wednesday Thursday Friday Saturday	9 oz. oatmeal 1 oz. rice 1 oz. Indian meal } Made into stirabout. 1 pint milk. ¼ lb. bread.		
Monday Wednesday Friday	} A.	Milk, 1 pint. Bread, 1½ lb. From 1st January to 1st July.	
Monday Wednesday Friday	} B.	Milk, 1 pint. Bread, ¼ lb. Potatoes, 2 lbs. From 1st July to 1st January.	
Tuesday Thursday Saturday		Beef, cooked, ½ lb. Soup, 1 pint. Potatoes, 1½ lbs.	

Ingredients to each Ration.

Soup.—To every pint of the liquor in which the meat is cooked add 1 oz. vegetables and 1 oz. oatmeal, with pepper and salt to them.

Tea.—To every pint, ½ oz. tea, ½ oz. sugar, and ½ pint milk.

Coffee.—To every pint, ½ oz. coffee, ⅛ oz. chicory, 1½ oz. molasses, and ½ pint milk.

(F.)

SCALE of Ordinary Prison Diet for Invalid Prisoners in Maryborough Convict Prison.

Breakfast.

12 oz. of bread and a pint of cocoa, consisting of ½ oz. cocoa, 1 oz. sugar, and ¼ pint new milk.

Dinner.

Sundays, Tuesdays, Thursdays, and Saturdays.

1 lb. of potatoes, ½ lb. of coarser parts of beef, boiled into a pint of soup, with ½ oz. of onions and 1 oz. of pearl barley to each pint.

Mondays, Wednesdays, and Fridays.

12 oz. bread and a pint of coffee, consisting of ½ oz. coffee, 1 oz. of sugar, and ¼ pint of new milk to each pint.

Supper.

8 oz. of bread and 1 pint of cocoa, made in same form as for breakfast.

Approved temporarily by their Excellencies
The Lords Justices.
6 February 1884.

General Prison Board,
10 February 1884.

Charles F. Bourke,
Chairman.

(G.)

SCALE of Sick Diets for Invalid Convicts in Maryborough Convict Prison.

No. 1 —3 pints of new milk, 3 pints of gruel, and 3 pints of tea.

No. 2.—BREAKFAST.—1 pint of arrowroot and pint of new milk.
    DINNER.—8 oz. of bread and a pint of broth made with ½ lb. of beef.
    SUPPER.—4 oz. of bread and 1 pint of tea.

No. 3.—BREAKFAST.—8 oz. of bread and 1 pint of new milk.
    DINNER.—4 oz. rice and 1 oz. of sugar boiled with 1 pint of new milk.
    SUPPER.—8 oz. of bread and 1 pint of new milk.

No. 4.—BREAKFAST.—8 oz. of bread and 1 pint of tea.
    DINNER.—1 lbs. of potatoes and ½ lb. of beef or mutton roast, and ½ oz. of
        onions, or 8 oz. beans boiled with 4 oz. cabbage every day save
        on Friday, when two eggs are given in lieu of meat.
    SUPPER.—8 oz. of bread and 1 pint of tea.

The Medical Officers are authorised to order such reasonable extras as they may consider necessary in special cases.

Ingredients.

¼ oz. of tea and ½ oz. of sugar with ⅟₁₀ pint of milk to each pint of tea.
2 oz. arrowroot and 1 oz. of sugar with a pint of new milk to each pint.
1 oz. of pearl barley and ½ oz. onions with pepper and salt to each pint of soup.
4 oz. of oatmeal to each pint of arrowroot.
2 oz. of oatmeal and 1 oz. of sugar to each pint of gruel.
½ oz. of coffee and 1 oz. of sugar to each pint, including ⅟₁₀ pint of milk.
½ oz. of shell cocoa and 1 oz. of sugar with ⅟₁₀ pint of new milk to each pint.

Approved by their Excellencies The Lords Justices.
    4 February 1886.

General Prisons Board, Dublin Castle,   Charles F. Bourke,
    10 February 1886.   Chairman.

PRISON RULES (IRELAND).

COPY of Rules and Regulations in force in
the Prisons in Ireland.

(Mr. John Ellis.)

Ordered, by The House of Commons, to be Printed,
7 August 1835.

[Price 10 d.]

329.   Under 8 oz.

www.ingramcontent.com/pod-product-compliance
Lightning Source LLC
Chambersburg PA
CBHW020252290326
41930CB00039B/1032